The Montgomery Bus Boycott and the Women Who Started It

The Montgomery Bus Boycott and the Women Who Started It

The Memoir of Jo Ann Gibson Robinson

Edited, with a Foreword, by David J. Garrow

The University of Tennessee Press

Frontispiece: Mrs. Jo Ann Gibson Robinson about 1974.

Library of Congress Cataloging-in-Publication Data

Robinson, Jo Ann Gibson, 1912–
  The Montgomery bus boycott and the women who
started it.

  Includes index.
  1. Segregation in transportation—Alabama—
Montgomery. 2. Robinson, Jo Ann Gibson, 1912–
3. Montgomery (Ala.)—Race relations. 4. Afro-
Americans—Civil rights—Alabama—Montgomery.
5. Afro-Americans—Alabama—Montgomery—Biography.
6. Montgomery (Ala.)—Biography. I. Garrow, David J.,
1953– . II. Title.
F334.M79N46 1987   976.1'47   86-14684
ISBN 0-87049-524-0 (alk. paper)

Contents

Illustrations

Harriet St.
Montgomery, Ala.
May 21, 1954

Copy of the letter sent to Mayor Gayle

Honorable Mayor W. A. Gayle
City Hall
Montgomery, Alabama

Dear Sir:

The Women's Political Council is very grateful to you and the City Commissioners for the hearing you allowed our representatives during the month of March, 1954, when the "city-bus-fare-increase case" was being reviewed. There were several things the Council asked for:

1. A city law that would make it possible for Negroes to sit from back toward front, and whites from front toward back until all the seats are taken:

2. That Negroes not be asked or forced to pay fare at front and go to the rear of the bus to enter:

3. That busses stop at every corner in residential sections occupied by Negroes as they do in communities where whites reside.

We are happy to report that busses have begun stopping at more corners now in some sections wher Negroes live then previously. However, the same practices in seating and boarding the bus continue.

Mayor Gayle, three-fourths of the riders of those public conveyances are Negroes. If Negroes did not patronize them, they could not possibly operate.

More and more of our people are already arranging with neighbors and friends to ride to keep from being insulted and humiliated by bus drivers.

There has been talk from twenty-five or more local organizations of planning a city-wide boycott of busses. We, sir, do not feel that forceful measures are necessary in bargaining for a convenience which is right for all bus passengers. We, the Council, believe that when this matter has been put before you and the Commissioners, that agreeable terms can be met in a quiet and unostensible manner to the satisfaction of all concerned.

Many of our Southern cities in neighboring states have practiced the policies we seek without incident whatsoever. Atlanta, Macon and Savannah in Georgia have done this for years. Even Mobile, in our own state, does this and all the passengers are satisfied.

Please consider this plea, and if possible, act favorably upon it, for even now plans are being made to ride less, or not at all, on our busses. We do not want this.

Respectfully yours,

The Women's Political Council

Jo Ann Robinson, President

Jo Ann Robinson's letter of 1954 to Mayor Gayle. Courtesy of Black Communications Group.

Foreword

David J. Garrow

I first met Mrs. Jo Ann Robinson in Los Angeles in April 1984 when I called to ask her if I could interview her about her crucial but little-heralded role in bringing about the Montgomery Bus Boycott of 1955–1956. The Montgomery boycott, which many scholars view as the first major event in the black freedom struggle of the 1950s and 1960s, has been highlighted in most textbook accounts of that era, in part because it propelled black Montgomery's spokesman, the Reverend Martin Luther King, Jr., to national prominence. Only one serious (and rather obscure) study, however, had looked at the real origins of the Montgomery protest. Some more general accounts went beyond Dr. King's role to note the important contributions of both Mrs. Rosa Parks, whose arrest for refusing to surrender her bus seat to a white man had kicked off the boycott, and E D. Nixon, a black Pullman porter and long-time Montgomery political activist, but only that single study ("Challenge and Response in the Montgomery Bus Boycott of 1955–56," *Alabama Review* 33, July 1980) by Professor J. Mills Thornton III had highlighted how, in the years preceding the boycott, the most active and assertive black civic group in Montgomery had been the Women's Political Council

Portions of this Foreword are drawn from the author's article, "The Origins of the Montgomery Bus Boycott," *Southern Changes* 7 (Oct.-Dec. 1985), published by the Southern Regional Council.

(WPC), headed by Mrs. Jo Ann Robinson, then a professor of English at Alabama State College.

My interest in Mrs. Robinson's and the WPC's role had been tremendously stimulated when, thanks to the helpfulness of Montgomery County District Attorney Johnny Evans, I had read through the files of documents accumulated in the mid-1950s by Evans' predecessor concerning the boycott and had come across the most remarkable sheet of paper I had ever seen in some eight years of research on the civil rights movement: a May 21, 1954, letter from Mrs. Robinson, on behalf of the WPC, to Montgomery Mayor W. A. "Tacky" Gayle insisting upon improved conditions for black riders of city buses and threatening a boycott if city and bus company officials did not offer significant improvements.

The letter was stunning in two respects: first, here was the strongest possible documentary evidence for strengthening and expanding Thornton's little-noted point that it had been this group of black women, and not simply or largely Parks, Nixon, King, and other ministers, who really had taken the lead in creating the Montgomery boycott. Second, the date of Mrs. Robinson's letter—four days after the Supreme Court had handed down its landmark ruling in *Brown* v. *Board of Education of Topeka*—was more than one and a half years *before* the actual boycott had gotten underway following Mrs. Parks's arrest on December 1, 1955. Clearly there was much more of a story, and a most historically-significant story, underlying this letter than most scholars of the black civil rights movement had even begun to realize.

Hence I had looked forward with considerable anticipation to talking with Mrs. Robinson, and when I called her to voice my request and explain my interest, she was more than eager to tell her story. Indeed, even though I was perfectly capable of getting myself to her house at whatever time might be most convenient for her, Mrs. Robinson insisted on driving over to where I was staying, at whatever time I wanted, to take me to her home—simply one example, I would come to learn, of the profoundly kind and friendly attitude Mrs. Robinson displayed toward virtually anyone whom she came to know.

I had the belief, stimulated perhaps by a comment someone

previously had made to me in Montgomery, that Mrs. Robinson at some earlier time had written out a substantial account of her experience in Montgomery, an account that had never been published or even privately circulated in typescript. I asked her about that as she drove me to her home, and she said yes, she had written such a manuscript, and she greatly hoped that somehow she could get it published. She had mentioned that desire, she said, to any number of acquaintances, some of whom had read her manuscript, but nothing had ever developed. Would I, she asked, be willing to try to help her get it published? I said I would be happy to look through it and to recommend it to an appropriate publisher if it had possibilities; privately, in my own mind, I feared that Mrs. Robinson's manuscript, like other unpublished autobiographical texts I had been shown in similar circumstances in previous years, might not be a credible candidate for publication.

Once we reached her house Mrs. Robinson sat me down on her living room couch and gave to me her more than two hundred page typescript titled "The Montgomery Story: Reflections on the Inside Story of the Bus Boycott That Set a People Free, 1955–1957." I started to look through it, skimming at first and then reading more closely as I began to realize just how much original, never-before-told historical detail there was about black civic activism in Montgomery prior to the boycott, about how she in particular, aided by several friends and a number of WPC colleagues, had taken the crucial actions in the hours immediately following Mrs. Parks's arrest to actually set a boycott in motion, and about the unproductive negotiations that subsequently took place between the black organization set up to pursue the boycott, the Montgomery Improvement Association (MIA), and white leaders.

Here indeed, I realized as I read further into her manuscript, was an autobiographical account that not only deserved publication, but that could be perhaps the most important participant-observer account of the Montgomery protest that students and scholars of the American black freedom struggle might ever have available.

As I became more engrossed with her manuscript, Mrs. Robinson insisted on fixing me lunch, and when we sat down to eat, I started asking her the many questions that my previous research and her manuscript had raised in my mind. That manuscript, I realized, even though a first-person, autobiographical story, showed Mrs. Robinson to be a resolutely self-effacing person, someone who was exceedingly reluctant to give to herself, rather than to others, credit for some accomplishment. As we talked, I could see that she was similarly very shy about highlighting her own life story.

Only with gentle but insistent encouragement, both during that long conversation and in subsequent correspondence, was I able to get Mrs. Robinson to tell me more about her early life. Jo Ann Gibson Robinson had moved to Montgomery in the late summer of 1949, at the age of thirty-three, to join the English department at Alabama State. She had been born in Culloden, Georgia, twenty-five miles from Macon, as the twelfth and youngest child of Owen Boston Gibson and Dollie Webb Gibson, land-owning black farmers who prospered until Owen Gibson died when Jo Ann was six years old. As the older children moved away, operating the farm grew more difficult for Mrs. Gibson, who eventually sold the property and moved into Macon with her younger offspring. Jo Ann graduated from the segregated, all-black high school there as the class valedictorian, and went on to earn her undergraduate degree at Fort Valley State College, the first member of her family to complete college. She took a public school teaching job in Macon and married Wilbur Robinson, but the marriage, heavily burdened by the death in infancy of their first and only child, lasted only a short time. Twelve months later, after five years of teaching in Macon, Jo Ann Robinson moved to Atlanta to take an M.A. in English at Atlanta University and then accepted a teaching position at Mary Allen College in Crockett, Texas. After one year there, Mrs. Robinson received a better offer from Alabama State, and moved to Montgomery.

With some further encouragement and questions, Mrs. Robinson recalled for me how she had been an enthusiastic teacher who had responded energetically to her new position at Alabama State. She also became an active member of Dexter Avenue Baptist Church, which many Alabama State professors attended, and she joined the Women's Political Council, a black professional women's civic group that one of her English department colleagues, Mrs.

Mary Fair Burks, had founded three years earlier when the local League of Women Voters had refused to integrate.

Those first months in Montgomery were a blissful fall semester, Mrs. Robinson remembered. "I loved every minute of it." How, though, I asked, did her initial membership in the WPC translate, within five years time, to that remarkable letter about bus conditions that she had written to Mayor Gayle in 1954? Although her manuscript narrated in some detail the political events leading up to the boycott, it was relatively silent, at least in its current form, about what her personal motivations might have been for becoming a leading community activist at a time and in a place where any manifestations of black dissent often resulted in white retribution, sometimes of a physical sort.

As Mrs. Robinson began to respond, her tone became more emotional and tears began to well up in her eyes. Just prior to her first Christmas in Montgomery, she explained, she got ready to visit some relatives in Cleveland for the holidays. On the appointed day she boarded a Montgomery City Lines public bus for the ride to Dannelly Field, the municipal airport. Only two other passengers were aboard, and Mrs. Robinson, immersed in her holiday thoughts, took a seat toward the front of the bus. Suddenly, however, she was roused from her thoughts about her family by angry words from the driver, who was ordering her to get up.

"He was standing over me, saying 'Get up from there! Get up from there,' with his hand drawn back," Mrs. Robinson told me.

Shaken and frightened, she fled from the bus. Ignorant of Montgomery's bus seating practices, she had made the mistake of sitting in one of the front ten seats that always were reserved for white riders. "I felt like a dog. And I got mad, after this was over, and I realized that I was a human being, and just as intelligent and far more trained than that bus driver was. But I think he wanted to hurt me, and he did . . . I cried all the way to Cleveland."

That experience convinced her, Mrs. Robinson recalled for me, that the Women's Political Council ought to target Montgomery's segregated bus seating for immediate attention. "It was then that I made up . . . my mind that whatever I could add to that organization that would help to bring that practice down, I would do it," she explained. "When I came back, the first thing I did was to call a meeting . . . and tell them what had happened."

Only then did Mrs. Robinson learn that her experience was far from unique, that dozens of other black citizens, primarily women, had suffered similar abuse from Montgomery bus drivers over the years. It was from those experiences, she explained, that she and her WPC colleagues were so strongly motivated to pursue the issue of bus seating conditions in the years leading up to 1955–1956.

Touched as well as enlightened by the emotional remembrance my question had drawn from Mrs. Robinson, I explained to her that yes, her manuscript had definite possibilities for publication, most probably by a scholarly press with a particular interest in southern history, but that it would benefit from some changes, such as the addition of such personally compelling stories about her own feelings during those years as the one she had just related to me. Given her role in the Montgomery story, I said, she should not combine her already self-effacing nature with a further effort to be "objective" or too distant from her narrative; instead, she should not hesitate to admit frankly to her readers just how central and highly motivated a participant she had been in the historically-crucial but often little-reported events of those years.

Mrs. Robinson eagerly voiced her willingness to make whatever improvements would strengthen her account, and with her permission I made inquiry of two southern scholarly presses to ask if they would be interested in publishing her account and in working with her to help strengthen it. Both responded favorably, and Mrs. Robinson voiced a preference for allowing the University of Tennessee Press to read her manuscript first.

In the actual publication of this book, the greatest debt is owed to Mavis Bryant, then the acquisitions editor at the University of Tennessee Press, who responded with great enthusiasm when she read Mrs. Robinson's story and who devoted literally hundreds of hours to helping craft it into its present form by counseling Mrs. Robinson to rearrange some portions, to add accounts of personal experiences such as that 1949 incident on the way to Dannelly Field, and to trim some sections where her narrative had moved away from the Montgomery story itself. After Ms. Bryant and Mrs. Robinson had completed these revisions, both Professor Thornton and myself read through the manuscript and recommended a modest number of changes for reasons of more general historical accuracy, most of which have been incorporated into the text.

Now over seventy years of age, Jo Ann Gibson Robinson lives quietly by herself in retirement in Los Angeles. Looking back at the Montgomery boycott, she still marvels at her initial surprise over white officials' absolute refusal to grant any of the boycotters' initially modest demands. "They feared that anything they gave would be viewed by us as just a start," she observed. "And you know, they were probably right."

Mrs. Robinson remains generally hesitant to claim for herself the historical credit that she deserves for launching the Montgomery Bus Boycott of 1955–1956. Although her story fully and accurately describes how it was she, during the night and early morning hours of December 1 and 2, 1955, who actually started the boycott on its way, it is only with some gentle encouragement that she will acknowledge herself as "the instigator of the movement to start the boycott." Even then, however, she seeks to emphasize that no special credit ought to go to herself or to any other single individual. Very simply, she says, "the black women did it." And as you will see, she's right.

The Memoir of
Jo Ann Gibson Robinson

Dedication

Boycotting taught me courage. The memory of the thousands of boycotters, walking in hot and cold weather, in rain,
sleet, and sunshine, for thirteen long months, makes me feel
ever so humble. These people inspired me to refuse to accept
what was wrongfully imposed upon me. Justice in the end
was the coveted goal that helped and inspired me and fifty
thousand others to become involved. Their suffering cannot
possibly be adequately told. These are the people who sac-
rificed. The people did it! Thus, this book is dedicated to
them—*the people!*

This book must also recognize the key role of the black
ministers of Montgomery. The memory of their leadership
will last forever. God bless them and keep them!

I also dedicate this work to all those men and women who
gave rides to the boycotting thousands who walked to make
a people free, especially three women drivers: Mrs. A. W.
West, Mrs. Alberta James, and Mrs. Daisy Poole.

Finally, this book is dedicated to the memory of my mother
and father, Owen Boston Gibson and Dollie Webb Gibson,
both of whom are deceased; to the memory of all six of my
brothers, who have entered into another expression; and to
my five sisters, three of whom survive.

We wear the mask that grins and lies,
It hides our cheeks and shades our eyes,
This debt we pay to human guile;
With torn and bleeding hearts we smile,
And mouth with myriad subtleties.

Why should the world be over-wise,
In counting all our tears and sighs?
Nay, let them only see us, while
We wear the mask.

We smile, but, O great Christ, our cries
To thee from tortured souls arise.
We sing, but oh the clay is vile
Beneath our feet, and long the mile;
But let the world dream otherwise,
We wear the mask!

—Paul Laurence Dunbar (1872–1906),
"We Wear the Mask," from *Complete Poems*
(Dodd-Mead, 1913)

Preface

Montgomery, Alabama!

Third largest city in the state, and once the capital of the Confederacy of the eleven southern states that waged the Civil War against the rest of the United States. The home of Big Jim Folsom, once-powerful governor of Alabama, and also of controversial Governor George Wallace, who suffered the bullet of a would-be assassin that left him a cripple and virtually an invalid.

Montgomery, whose state capital buildings sit high on a hill, overlooking the beautiful southern city below, pierced by its main artery, Dexter Avenue. Dexter audaciously and conspicuously provides space for the Dexter Avenue Baptist Church for black people, where Dr. Martin Luther King, Jr., leader of the 1955–1956 Montgomery Bus Boycott, served as pastor.

Dr. King and I often discussed the probability that Montgomery was the only city that a boycott could have thrived in. For Montgomery was a college town. Alabama State College was an institution of which the black masses took advantage. It did not take in all the masses, but the so-called "upper crust" graduated from college with degrees. They were well read. Parents worked days and went to college nights. Children went to college because the college was there. The effect on attitudes was amazing: few inferiority complexes, no fear of "whitey," great faith in self, in families, and in people. A college town develops attitudes of defiance against discrimination, and people there are less prone to succumb to force. It also cultivates desires for learning and generates some philosophic depth.

Even so, in Montgomery, before December 5, 1955, thousands of black citizens gave every impression of being willing to go on enduring discrimination on buses, suffering humiliation and embarrassment, for the sake of peace. In the words of the poet Paul Laurence Dunbar, they wore "the mask that grins and lies" to hide their hurt feelings. Many white people thought blacks were a "happy-go-lucky" people. Although blacks felt they were being deprived of their rights, they endured nevertheless, complacent and tolerant, though dreading every occasion on which they had to accept the treatment they received on buses. They complained and grumbled among themselves but kept on enduring, riding the monsters for the sake of peace.

The bus boycott originated in the demeaning, wretched, intolerable impositions and conditions that black citizens experienced in a caste system commonly called segregation. The segregated bus system had existed for over half a century. Although from the beginning protests had been registered repeatedly, black people had had no choice. The system confined them, but it could not obliterate their bitterness, humiliation, and anger. They were determined to get an education, to become financially secure, so that when the time came they would be prepared to walk away from the system. And on December 5, 1955, fifty thousand people—the generally estimated black population—walked off public city buses in defiance of existing conditions which were demeaning, humiliating, and too intolerable to endure.

For thirteen months they refused to ride those carriers, until conditions had been changed to meet their approval. And in December 1956, thirteen long months after the bus boycott began, the federal courts ordered the buses integrated, and buses began operating without segregation or discrimination.

About the Author

I was born in Georgia, the twelfth and last child of Owen Boston Gibson and Dollie Webb Gibson. I recall very vividly my mother and father and my eleven sisters and brothers; we were six boys and six girls. I was the sixth girl. By the time I was six years old, my father had died. My older sisters and brothers began to marry and move away. Soon only a few of us girls remained with my mother on the farm, and my mother had to hire some help to carry on as usual. All schools in rural areas were closed when "cotton-pickin' time" drew near. After the harvest, schools reopened, and children went back to school.

However, my brother Van, fourth from the oldest of the twelve, bought a large house in Macon, Georgia, and prevailed on my mother to sell the plantation and livestock and move in with him. She complied, and all of us left in tears. We all entered school and graduated from high school at different times. I was the only one of the twelve who went on to college and graduate school. The others, one by one, got married and moved out.

I graduated from high school as valedictorian, and with good recommendations from teachers that won me scholarships, I graduated from college, earning a B.S. degree from Georgia State College at Fort Valley. I taught in the public school system of Macon, and got married. But the loss of a child made me very bitter, and the marriage did not last. A year later I went back to graduate school at Atlanta University for an M.A. degree in English and literature. I also completed one year's work in the doctoral program in English at Teachers College, Columbia University, New York City. After moving to Los Angeles, California, I did one semester at the University of Southern California.

My first experience teaching on the college level was at Mary Allen College in Crockett, Texas. The college's president, Dr. Prince, offered me the chairmanship of the English department, and I enthusiastically accepted. Dr. Prince, whom everybody loved, was most helpful to new teachers, and teaching there was a rewarding experience. The next year, Dr. H. Councill Trenholm, president of Alabama State College in Montgomery, offered me a position in the

English department at Alabama State, and I accepted, beginning in the fall of 1949.

On one single day in 1949, I met many of the people who were to play such important roles in my life and the lives of all black Americans in the years to come: future attorney Fred Gray and his wife Bernice; Dr. Trenholm's wife Portia; Dr. Mary Fair Burks, president of the Women's Political Council (WPC); and other teachers who were WPC members. I liked them all. That day I joined the WPC. Later I succeeded Dr. Burks as president of this organization, which was to start the Montgomery Bus Boycott. We women prepared the notices calling riders off the buses. We distributed those notices, and then, when the ministers took over, we worked with them until the very end.

In addition to being WPC president, I was a member of the Executive Board of the Montgomery Improvement Association (MIA) and editor of the monthly *MIA Newsletter* that went to people around the globe. During the course of the boycott, I served on all of the major committees, at Dr. King's request. I was one of the persons arrested in the course of the boycott; that was my first direct experience of what takes place when people are incarcerated.

In general, however, I kept a low profile and stayed as much as possible in the background. That I did so was not from fear for my own well-being, but rather out of deep respect for Dr. Trenholm, for Alabama State College, and for its faculty and student body—all of whom would have been unavoidably implicated in case of trouble.

Why I Am Writing This Book

I have chosen to record the facts of the Montgomery Bus Boycott for several reasons. The first is general: so that the world will know that black people of America are not, as stereotypes have depicted them for generations, a "happy-go-lucky," self-satisfied, complacent, lazy, good-for-nothing race that has nothing good or worthwhile to offer society. People the world over should know that any group, if given equal opportunity in education, employment, civil rights, and the like, can be desirable citizens anywhere, with as much (and in some cases more) to offer as any other group. Debasement or degeneracy of character is not confined to one race, but is found in all races. From this record future generations may know that black Americans are just people like other people, wanting the same things, doing the same things, enduring the same things, and fighting against the same things that destroy the soul as well as the mind and body. When this is understood, a pure democratic government may survive in the American land of freedom, with justice and opportunity for all.

The second reason I have for writing this book is specific: to show that black Americans can endure hardship and suffering for the cause of justice. If given the same chance to get an education and to obtain jobs on all levels for which they are trained, oppressed people can control emotion and discipline feeling, even when tension is high and justice is derelict.

Third, I have attempted to relate the verifiable truth in every area of concern, so that the reader will know *why* fifty thousand black citizens walked off city transit lines and refused to patronize them again for thirteen long months, until they were integrated. They just could not take any more abuse!

Finally, I want to leave to our posterity an accurate account of a struggle for justice in the Deep South, staged by an oppressed but brave people, whose pride and dignity rose to the occasion, conquered fear, and faced whatever perils had to be confronted. The boycott was the most beautiful memory that all of us who participated will carry to our final resting place. Black Americans' children and their children's children have the right to know about the struggle of their forebears, in helping to make this country beautiful for all its people—beautiful in terms of equality of opportunity, human dignity, and self-respect.

Sources

Everything that is told in these pages has been experienced by this writer, or provided by individual participants who related their personal accounts to me and to others who were interested in recording the facts for posterity, or reported in newspapers and other media.

I took many notes in official meetings, when I was a part of the negotiation committees at city hall. The account of my encounters with police officers who "booked" me during my arrest is also personal. These encounters gave me an inside experience that I value highly. I can understand the personal frustrations those police officers must have felt, while they were only doing their duty. They are human, too!

When I gave boycotters rides during my hours off from work, they told me of their personal experiences. I have tried to recapture here the feelings of those bus riders as they related to me their humiliating personal ordeals at the hands of individual bus drivers.

Finally, many things in this book have appeared in newspapers, magazines, books, or on television from time to time. I have tried to verify my records and memories against such sources.

Acknowledgments

Indebtedness is acknowledged for the various testimonies given me by people to whom I gave rides during the long months of the boycott.

Mrs. Geraldine Nesbitt, a retired public school teacher in Montgomery, was kind enough to send me many clippings from the *Montgomery Advertiser* and the *Alabama Journal,* two local newspapers that provided excellent coverage of the bus boycott in 1955–1956. The clippings helped to substantiate materials used in this book. Without Mrs. Nesbitt's assistance, this writing would have been incomplete. For her help I am most grateful.

Miss Willie Mae (Billie) Robinson, a retired teacher in Birmingham, Alabama, and my very good friend, supplied invaluable clippings of events in Birmingham.

Miss Doris Howard, a vice principal of the Los Angeles public schools, who offered critical judgment, was most helpful. Her criticisms and suggestions were well received and appreciated.

Professor Thomas Hunt, a former colleague of mine in the Los Angeles school system, and now a transportation specialist with the California Public Utilities Commission, offered critical judgment and literary suggestions that were invaluable. His criticisms contributed much to the merits of this work.

Mrs. Fannie Motley, my neighbor, supplied me with at least one important clipping, for which I am grateful.

Dr. Archie Lacey, formerly of Alabama State University but now professor of science education at Herbert H. Lehman College, City University of New York, encouraged and inspired me to write this book.

Finally, thanks to my own family, whose tolerance and endurance during the wee hours of the night or early morning, when typewriter keys played havoc with their sleep, helped so much.

Prologue

I was as happy as I had ever been in my life that Saturday morning before Christmas in December 1949 as I prepared to leave the campus of Alabama State College in Montgomery for the holidays. I had been a member of the English faculty at the college since September of that year, and I had loved every minute of it.

Dr. H. Councill Trenholm, the college president, was a wonderful administrator, and his carefully selected staff of well-trained teachers and the college's eager students filled my life with gratitude that I was a part of it all.

One of the men students loaded my suitcases in my car for me, and I drove at a leisurely pace out to the airport, checked my luggage for the trip to the East, then returned to the college campus, locked my car in a garage, made my way to the nearest bus stop, and waited for the short ride to a friend's home. We were all going to the airport together. I had never felt freer or happier.

I boarded an almost empty city bus, dropped my coins into the proper place, and observed the passengers aboard, only two—a white woman who sat in the third row from the front, and a black man in a seat near the back. I took the fifth row seat from the front and sat down, immediately closing my eyes and envisioning, in my mind's eye, the wonderful two weeks' vacation I would have with my family and friends in Ohio.

From the far distance of my reverie I thought I heard a voice, an unpleasant voice, but I was too happy to worry about voices, or any noise for that matter. But the same words were repeated, in a stronger, unsavory tone, and I opened my eyes. Immediately I sat up in that seat. The bus driver had stopped the bus, turned in his seat, and was speaking to me!

"If you can sit in the fifth row from the front of the other buses in Montgomery, suppose you get off and ride in one of them!" I heard him, but the message did not register with me. My thoughts were elsewhere. I had not even noticed that the bus had come to a full stop, or I had subconsciously surmised that passengers were getting on or off.

Suddenly the driver left his seat and stood over me. His hand was drawn back as if he were going to strike me. "Get up from there!" he yelled. He repeated it, for, dazed, I had not moved. "Get up from there!"

I leaped to my feet, afraid he would hit me, and ran to the front door to get off the bus. I even stepped down to the lower level, so that when the door was opened, I could step off the bus and hide myself, for tears were falling rapidly from my eyes. It suddenly occurred to me that I was supposed to go to the back door to get off, not the front! However, I was too upset, frightened, and tearful to move. I never could have walked to the rear door. Then the driver opened the front door, and I stumbled off the bus and started walking back to the college. Tears blinded my vision; waves of humiliation inundated me; and I thanked God that none of my students was on that bus to witness the tragic experience. I could have died from embarrassment.

My friends came and took me to the airport, but my holiday season was spoiled. I cried all the way to my destination and pretended to have a headache when my relatives met me at the airport in Cleveland five or six hours later. In all these years I have never forgotten the shame, the hurt, of that experience. The memory will not go away.

Even now, when segregation has been abolished and riders sit where they please on public transportation lines, memories like mine will not fade away. Although almost thirty years have gone by, black people have not forgotten the years leading up to the boycott of 1955—the suffering, the abuse they endured at the hands of arrogant white bus drivers. It was during the period of 1949–1955 that the Women's Political Council of Montgomery—founded in 1946 with Dr. Mary Fair Burks as president and headed from 1950 on by me—prepared to stage a bus boycott when the time was ripe and the people were ready. The right time came in 1955.

1

The Origin of the Trouble

It was Monday, December 5, 1955.

For Negroes and whites alike among the 120,000 people who made up Montgomery, Alabama, the working day was beginning, busy with early morning activity. Meteorologically speaking, the day was no different from other winter days in the South—it was cold, threatening to rain. This day was no different to a casual, indifferent observer, or to most of the thousands of white people who were more or less indifferent or partly amused observers. Perhaps the personnel of the Montgomery City Lines, Incorporated, were a little concerned, because even one unfavorable day could cause a serious reduction in bus fare receipts.

But to Montgomery's fifty thousand black citizens, the cold, cloudy December day *was* different. None of them had slept very well the night before, for they had not been quite sure that their group would really cooperate in the "one-day bus boycott" of city buses. Then there was the cold and the threat of rain, neither of which was in their favor. And they—sleepy, tense with glorious expectancy, hopeful, even prayerful that all of them would endure for one day—were afraid. They were afraid that their well-planned one-day protest against the Montgomery City Lines would fail, that blacks in large numbers would ride the buses, and that the proud black leaders of the boycott would be the laughingstock of the town.

There would not have been such fear of embarrassment if the

boycott plans had not been discovered by whites and publicized in radio and television broadcasts and in huge, black, glaring front-page headlines in local newspapers. But the city did know of their plans, and black people were on the spot.

At 5:30 A.M. Monday, December 5, dawn was breaking over Montgomery. Early morning workers were congregating at corners. There, according to the plan, Negroes were to be picked up not by the Montgomery City Lines, but by Negro taxis driving at reduced rates of ten cents per person, or by some two hundred private cars which had been offered free to bus riders for Monday only.

The suspense was almost unbearable, for no one was positively sure that taxi drivers would keep their promises, that private car owners would give absolute strangers a ride, that Negro bus riders would stay off the bus. And then there was the cold and the threat of rain!

The black Women's Political Council had been planning the boycott of Montgomery City Lines for months, but the plans had only been known publicly for the past three days. The idea itself had been entertained for years. Almost daily some black man, woman, or child had had an unpleasant experience on the bus and told other members of the family about it at the supper table or around the open fireplace or stove. These stories were repeated to neighbors, who re-told them in club meetings or to the ministers of large church congregations.

At first the ministers would soothe the anger of their congregations with recommendations of prayer, with promises that God would "make the rough ways smooth" and with exhortations to "have patience and wait upon the Lord."

The members had been patient and had waited upon the Lord, but the rough ways had gotten rougher rather than smoother. As months stretched into years, the encounters with some of the bus drivers grew more numerous and more intolerable.

Very little or nothing tangible had ever been done on the part of the darker race to prevent continuous abuse on city transit lines, except to petition the company and the City Commission for better conditions. Ten years before, when Mrs. Geneva Johnson, in the latest of a long string of similar incidents, was arrested for not having correct change and "talking back" to the driver when he upbraided her, nothing was done. Charged with disorderly conduct, she paid her fine and kept on riding. A representation of Negro men complained to the bus company about the matter and about other mistreatments as well, but nothing came of it.

During the next few years, Mrs. Viola White and Miss Katie Wingfield were arrested, as well as two children visiting from New Jersey. All had committed the same offense—sitting in the front seats reserved for whites. The children were a sister and brother, ten and twelve years old, respectively, who had been accustomed to riding integrated transportation. They got on the bus and sat down by a white man and a boy. The white youngster told the older black youth to get up from beside him. The youngster refused. The driver commanded them to move, but the children refused. The driver again commanded them to move, but the children continued to sit where they were. They were not in the habit of getting up out of their seats on a public vehicle to give them to somebody else. The police were called, and the two children were arrested. Relatives paid their fines, sent the children home, and the case became history. People kept on riding the bus, and, in all probability, those two children carried and will continue to carry that bitter experience with them forever.

Three years later, in 1952, a white bus driver and a Negro man exchanged words over the dime the passenger put into the slot. The Negro man, Brooks, was not afraid, for he had been drinking. He never quavered when the driver abused him with words and accused him of not putting the money into the meter box of the bus. Instead, he stood his ground and disputed the driver. The "bracer" gave him confidence to stand there, and to sit down, and to talk back in his own defense.

What followed was never explained fully, but the driver called the police, and when the police came they shot and killed Brooks as he got off the bus. Newspaper reports stated that the coroner had ruled the case justifiable homicide because the man had resisted arrest. Many black Montgomerians felt that Brooks was intoxicated and had gotten "out of his place" with the white bus driver. Others wondered if any man, drunk or sober, had to be killed because of one dime, one bus fare. Each had his own thoughts on the matter, but kept on riding the bus.

In 1953, Mrs. Epsie Worthy got on a bus at a transfer point from another bus, and the driver demanded an additional fare. He refused to take the transfer. Rather than pay again, the woman decided that she did not have far to go and would walk the rest of the way. The driver would not be daunted. He wanted another fare, whether she rode or got off, and insisted upon it. Words followed as the woman alighted from the vehicle. She was not quite quick enough, for by the time she was safe on mother earth, the driver was upon her, beating her with his hands. She defended herself, fighting back with all her might. For a few minutes there was a "free-for-all," and she gave as much as she took. But in the end she was the loser, for when the police were summoned, she was taken to jail and fined fifty-two dollars for disorderly conduct.

The Women's Political Council

In 1953, the members of the Women's Political Council (WPC) were confronted with some thirty complaints against the bus company, brought to it by black people in the community.

This organization of black women had been founded in 1946, nine years before the boycott began, by Dr. Mary Fair (Mrs. N. W. or "Frankye") Burks, chairman of the English department at Alabama State College. She became the WPC's first president, and it was she who organized the women who would work together as leaders and followers, giving and taking suggestions, and who would never reveal the secrets of the WPC. Dr. Burks, a profound scholar, highly intelligent and fearless, was a native Alabamian who had suffered from the segregated rules, the hypocrisy of race separation by day only. Pained by the suffering her people would continue to endure if things kept on as they were and had been from the beginning, Dr. Burks *knew* that one day, when human beings had taken all they could digest, the fight would begin. Thus, her thoughts gave birth to the WPC of college women and those who lived in the area.

Historians have written that women—white, black, and in-between—are the men's power structure of the universe. If there had not been women, there would not have been men, and vice versa. And there is the hidden secrct that when the curtains of darkness fall, and the sun transports its sunlight into darkness, color is insignificant. Proof of it is in the variegated colors of human beings—white, black, red, yellow, brown—whose physical structures are normally identical.

The WPC was formed for the purpose of inspiring Negroes to live above mediocrity, to elevate their thinking, to fight juvenile and adult delinquency, to register and vote, and in general to improve their status as a group. We were "woman power," organized to cope with any injustice, no matter what, against the darker sect.

In Montgomery in 1955, no one was brazen enough to announce publicly that black people might boycott city buses for the specific purpose of *integrating* those buses. Just to say that minorities wanted "better seating arrangements" was bad enough. That was the term the two sides, white and black, always used later in discussing the boycott. The word "integration" never came up. Certainly all blacks knew not to use that word while riding the bus. To admit that black Americans were seeking to integrate would have been too much; there probably would have been much bloodshed and arrests of those who dared to disclose such an idea! That is why, during the boycott negotiations to come, the Men of Montgomery and other organizations always said that blacks would sit from back toward front, and whites would sit from the front of the bus toward the back, until all seats were taken.

The WPC, however, knew all the time that black Americans were working for integration, pure and simple. No front toward back, or vice versa! We knew we were human beings; that neither whites nor blacks were responsible for their color; that someday those buses, of necessity, had to be integrated; and that after integration neither would be worse off. For both were human; both were clean. And Montgomery, a college town, was capable of integrating, if each side would consider the matter seriously, without prejudice, and decide what was best for all concerned—the bus company, the white population, and the black population. We were, then, bent on integration. There were those afraid to admit it. But, we knew that deep down in the secret minds of all—teachers, students, and community—black Americans wanted integration. That way we would achieve equality. The only way.

The early WPC members all lived in the general neighborhood of the college. Most were professional women. There were competent educators, supervisors, principals, teachers, social workers, other community workers, nurses—women employees from every walk of life. Many of the women from Alabama State College were members; so were many public school teachers. It must be remembered that the women of the WPC were laying their "all" on the line in organizing themselves to defeat segregation in the heart of the Confederacy.

One hundred members was the limit for one group. However, there were so many requests for membership that a second chapter was organized to cover another part of the city. Soon a third group had to be organized, as furious women realized that everybody had to become involved if black Americans were to win their fight, put the bus company out of business, and integrate those carriers or establish a transportation system of their own. By 1955, then, the WPC had three chapters distinguished as Group 1 (the original group), Group 2, and Group 3.

The three divisions that resulted were organized in three different sections of the city and formed one of the best communication systems needed for operation of the boycott. Each group had its own officers—president, secretary, treasurer, telephone coordinators. The three chapter presidents were given all the information of an "expected" boycott, and were kept informed. Each group played a part in the distribution of the notices that called riders off city transportation lines. The three presidents kept in close touch with each other, and each president passed the news on to her group's members.

I followed Dr. Burks as head of the organization in 1950. When Mary Burks asked me to accept the leadership of the main chapter of the WPC, I readily accepted. I had suffered the most humiliating experience of my life when that bus driver had ordered me off the fifth row seat from the front and threatened to strike me when I did not move fast enough. Thus, I was ready to take over the WPC when the time came.

When I became president of the college chapter of the WPC, I called Mayor W. A. Gayle, told him who I was and the organization I represented, and requested an audience with him and the other two city commissioners. At that time the City Commission was composed of Mayor Gayle, George Cleere, and Dave Birmingham. After that first year, Frank Parks replaced Cleere, and Clyde Sellers won Birmingham's post. When I called, Mayor Gayle and his two colleagues readily agreed to receive three WPC officers in his office.

We found the mayor to be a very pleasant person, very likeable, easy to approach, and sincere in working with us. He had listened patiently to our requests to be allowed to attend his conferences with his staff, and to help solve nuisance problems where black people were concerned. He amicably agreed. Every time a meeting was held that involved minority groups, or issues that touched all Montgomery, he instructed his secretary to call. Six WPC representatives, including officers, always attended such meetings. I would always go; so did Dr. Burks. The other members attended when their schedules permitted. Members who were available went with us, and we all learned something from these experiences.

And we worked! We made suggestions that were accepted, and we often followed through on the solutions, which otherwise would have been left to the mayor's committee to implement. This relationship, when the WPC worked amicably with the mayor's office, existed for several years. Only when the struggle for integration on buses began did the friendship end. No longer did members of the WPC attend city hall meetings, for that privilege was no longer offered.

Meanwhile, the WPC began to gain popularity among black people. Since the WPC worked in community projects, sponsoring Youth City among high school seniors to train them in government and also sponsoring projects to encourage adults to become qualified voters, the community people came to the WPC for advice on many of their civic problems. Complaints came from people who were tired of abuse, wherever it occurred. It was during the 1954–1955 period, when complaints multiplied, that the WPC prepared to stage a bus boycott when the time was ripe and the people were ready.

Six years had gone by since I had become a teacher at Alabama State College. It was September 1955 now, and teachers at the college were gradually returning from their vacations to begin their fall classes. I, too, returned and immediately began plans for English and literature classes. Very soon everybody was at work as usual, and the weeks seemed to stretch into months as time hurried by.

However, for some strange reason, my mind kept turning to that first year when I had come to Montgomery and had the bitter experience of being forced to get up out of a seat on a public city transit line, in the most humiliating circumstances, with only two other passengers aboard, because that seat happened to be in a section reserved for white passengers. I had never forgotten that ordeal. I had not told it to anybody, not even my closest friends, because I was ashamed for anybody to know. Yet I could not rid my mind, my thoughts, my memory, of it! For the past six years the ache of that experience had been smoldering inside me. Far down in the recesses of my memory, it festered—a deep hurt that would not heal. It was consuming me! Yet, why I was remembering it so vividly now, I did not know. It had been six years ago, but it seemed as yesterday! The anger and shame inundated me as if it had happened just the day before.

Suddenly I realized that *six whole years* had gone by. Yet not one thing had been done to improve the conditions under which black citizens were forced by law to ride public transportation lines. And here I was *still* remembering that terrible experience and lamenting the fact that it had happened, not only to me but to so many hundreds, even thousands of other black Americans, young and old, men and women, girls and boys! All human beings. And similar situations were still happening. Six years and no improvement! Black Americans were still being treated as animals, things without feelings, not human beings!

"How long will this go on?" I asked myself aloud, and was startled when the answer came as though someone else was in the room. The answer seemed to come from all corners and from many voices: "As long as black Americans will allow it!" I turned and looked to see if anyone else was in the room, but I knew I was alone.

In my calmer moments, I knew that the bus company was not responsible for the law under which it operated, and that the company had, of necessity, to obey the authority of the three city commissioners. The City Fathers, in turn, were in office because of the voters—the white voters of Montgomery. At that time, very few black people of Montgomery were registered to vote. Thus, there was no one to whom black citizens could appeal.

"What must we do? What *can* we do?" I asked, half aloud, half to myself. And the answer seemed to come from everywhere at once: "Boycott! Boycott! Boycott! BOYCOTT!" I did not have the slightest idea how—without involving others who might get hurt— to begin a boycott against the bus company that would put that company out of business. But the Women's Political Council took the idea under advisement.

In 1955, while complaints came in to the WPC, others were being sent to other civic organizations, demanding that action be taken to improve conditions. The masses of blacks, incapable of defending themselves, wanted competent people of their race to intercede with proper officials for better treatment on transportation lines and other public facilities. They were mumbling among themselves with much disquietude.

While the WPC deliberated upon the best approach, two well-known organizations chaired by men, but whose membership included women as well as men, became extremely busy. The Progressive Democratic Association and the Citizens' Steering Committee attempted to hold a conference with the bus company to complain of the practices employed by bus drivers in connection with Negro riders. The WPC was informed that neither had been successful in obtaining a meeting with bus company officials. Therefore, they were unable to effect any improvement in the general practice of bus operators.

The Progressive Democratic Association, of which Mr. E. D. Nixon was president, was an old, well-established organization of black leaders, men and women. Some of the best political minds in Montgomery were in this group.

Mr. Nixon was well known throughout the city, county, and much of the state of Alabama and was highly respected by white and black citizens alike. He had a deep commanding voice, and people listened when he spoke. He had a great sense of humor, too, and loved to take the conversation while crowds listened to him. His happiest moments seemed to be those in which he was the center of attention, surrounded by people listening to him tell of his latest escapades with the law on behalf of suffering humanity.

In Montgomery, Mr. Nixon was a vital force to be reckoned with. In addition to being president of the Progressive Democratic Association, a leader of the Brotherhood of Sleeping Car Porters and a former president of the local and state branches of the National Association for the Advancement of Colored People, he had been a leader in the "human rights" movement for many years prior to the boycott. Although he lacked formal training, Nixon was acquainted with most of the members of the police and sheriff's departments, with the judges and jailers, and with people at city hall. Also he knew most of the lawyers in the city, white and black, and when he appealed to them for help for others who were in trouble, they often went to the rescue. They knew him, and they did not let him down.

When violations of human rights occurred, the victims involved would telephone Mr. Nixon, and he would go to their rescue. In fact, anytime a black citizen was arrested in the city and knew not whom to call for help in getting free, Mr. Nixon was called, often during the night, and he would go to city hall and get the prisoner out on bail. If a black person had been arrested on what amounted to a misdemeanor, Mr. Nixon could often get him freed or exonerated just by going to the place of incarceration. If the trouble was more serious, he knew what to do and whom to call to bring about a solution to the problem. If he had to, he would take a lawyer with him to get arrested persons out of jail. He posted bond for many and accepted responsibility for those who were released in his care. He might or might not know the person who called upon him for such favors, and he might or might not know her or his financial situation, but that did not stop him. He was a friend to all who were in trouble and appealed to him for help. He simply seemed to get pleasure out of helping people, especially those who could not help themselves.

Mr. Rufus Lewis, president of the Citizens' Steering Committee, fought in an entirely different way. His organization saw to it that people registered to vote as soon as their age level permitted.

Mr. Lewis was a businessman with experience in many fields of endeavor. There was nothing in the business world that he was not familiar with, and he always answered questions of those persons who were trying to get ahead in the world. He created his own jobs, for he had a number of business projects. He, his lovely wife Jewell, and their children were well known, well educated, and highly respected in Montgomery. The Lewises were believed to be quite wealthy, but they never flaunted their wealth. Many times Mr. Lewis drove an old rusty automobile that looked like it might collapse any time, but everybody knew that he had better cars.

Mr. Lewis' greatest joy was getting people registered to vote. For years he had worked faithfully with his race, encouraging every person twenty-one years old and older to become registered voters. His philosophy on voting was often expressed as: "A voteless people is a hopeless people." He often said that if enough black voters had been registered, the present city administrators, who were strong segregationists, would never have been elected. Any man who did not have a voter registration card Mr. Lewis considered not worthy of his time. For a man was not a man, he felt, until he became a registered voter. "Your power is at the ballot-box," Mr. Lewis used to tell young people, and some of them listened while others smiled and kept on their way.

He had a paid group of helpers, whose responsibility was getting eligible people registered. Working with him was Miss Idessa Williams, one of his faithful employees. Through the efforts of Mr. Lewis and Miss Williams, many young people became registered voters when they reached the legal age, and they encouraged others to do the same. She organized youth groups to make door-to-door, block-by-block investigations. Among the young people working in these groups were Mrs. Ethel Alexander, Ms. Viola Bradford, Mrs. Hattie Carter, Mrs. Gloria Jean German, Ms. Delores Glover,

Mr. Leon Hall (later of the Southern Christian Leadership Conference), Mrs. Bertha Howard and family, Ms. Yvonne Jenkins, Ms. Gwendolyn Patton, Ms. Bertha Smith, and Ms. Barbara Williams.

Mr. Lewis provided a Voter Registration Service booth near the college, conveniently located for student service. Those students who did not register had no excuse. His voter-education program was well known. Anywhere he met or came in contact with an unregistered adult, the verbal teaching began. Many voters said that they registered to "get Mr. Lewis off their backs."

He was persistent and never gave up. His work in the voting arena was in progress when I went to Alabama State College in 1949, and it was just as forceful, if not more so, when I left in 1960, eleven years later. Even when the bus boycott proved effective and black people were finally working together as one operative group, Mr. Lewis was not satisfied. He was impatient; black peers were too slow in getting themselves registered as voters. Some of them had children over twenty years old, but they were not registered yet, nor were their children. He could not understand what these unregistered "grown-ups" were waiting for. He and his group had registered many, but not enough, and even after integration of the buses, he continued to push his voter registration team to work harder to get all walking people to register and become eligible to vote. These efforts slowly began to become effective, for the black registered voters grew in numbers, and the power of more black voters began to take effect. Slowly, Mr. Lewis' dream began to be realized.

Since the Progressive Democratic Association and the Citizens' Steering Committee had failed to make contact with the bus company officials, the wpc leaders decided to seek an audience with the bus company. At the same time, Dr. Martin Luther King and a few other ministers of local churches had obtained a conference with city hall officials. I called Dr. King, and he invited three of us from the wpc to attend the conference.

We presented written and signed reports to the City Commission, pointing out drivers, bus numbers, hours, and routes when certain incidents occurred. Mrs. Thelma Glass and, if memory serves, Mrs. Jewell Lewis accompanied me. Both ladies were sharp, asked a deluge of questions, and pressed the commissioners for answers. After hearing our report, the commissioners promised an immediate investigation. In the meantime, conditions continued. Many black people, men in particular, started walking.

Not long after the WPC's visit to the commission, the bus company requested permission from the City Commission to increase bus fares, since patronage was diminishing. A public hearing was held on the matter. WPC representatives went to that meeting and protested the increase of fares, not because we were unwilling to pay for service rendered, but because we objected to the type of service, coupled with inhuman indignities, that was being given black people.

Among the things itemized in our protest were:

1. Continuous discourtesies with obscene language, especially name-calling in addressing black patrons.
2. Buses stopped at each block in neighborhoods where whites lived, but at every two blocks or block and a half in black neighborhoods.
3. Bus drivers' requirement that Negro passengers pay fares at the front of the bus, then step down off and walk to the back door to board the bus. The practice was a dangerous one, for people standing in the aisle blocked the view of the driver so that it was possible to catch a rider in the door and drag him a distance without knowing that he was there. In many instances the driver drove away before the patrons who had paid at the front could board the bus from the rear.
4. That the front ten double seats on each bus (out of a total seating for thirty-six) were reserved for whites, whether there were enough whites riding the bus to occupy them or not. Even when no whites were aboard, those seats were reserved, just in case one or two did ride. In many instances black riders had to stand over those empty seats. Since about 70 percent of all bus patrons were black, especially on certain buses and in certain areas, it seemed to many riders that the reservation of seats was unnecessary.

A delegation of five WPC members, including myself, made an appointment to speak with Mr. J. H. Bagley, the bus company manager. He was courteous, friendly, and very pleased that we had come. He informed us that he merely managed the company; that he had no jurisdiction over the city government and its laws; that he would request that Mr. K. E. Totten, the national company vice president who administered transit bus lines all over the country, come and speak with us.

We also conferred with Mayor Gayle and complained about the treatment black patrons were receiving on city transit lines. He was friendly; he explained the city laws of segregation that the bus company drivers had to conform to, but he was not opposed to Mr. Totten's visit. He did add that if dissatisfied bus patrons were not satisfied, they could always drive their own cars! Seemingly pleased that Mr. Totten was being invited and would bear a part of the responsibility of segregation, he bade us adieu with a smile and left us feeling that he was a very pleasant person.

In a few days, the mayor requested that drivers be more courteous and instructed the company to begin stopping at each block in areas occupied by black riders and to admit all passengers at the front door, except those who had large packages in their arms. Then, with the consent of the other two commissioners, he gave the company permission to increase fares from three tokens for a quarter, to ten cents straight for adults and five cents for school children. Transfers were to be given free.

The very next day buses stopped at each block over the entire city, and black riders felt proud and happy that the City Fathers had acted favorably in their behalf. For a few days bus operators acted in a generally satisfactory manner toward all passengers, and everyone was pleased. But the joy was short-lived. The mumblings started again, as stories of unhappy experiences began to circulate once more.

First, a group of men who had paid their fares at the front door were requested to step off the vehicle and go to the back to get on, so that they would not have to "walk over whites" to seats in the rear of the bus. They did so, but before they could board at the rear, the driver drove off leaving them standing on the sidewalk. They were not merely psychologically blocked with the "back door" stigma, but they were "short of change" and still had to get to work.

At Holt Street and Jeff Davis Avenue, a mentally defective but harmless black man, after walking in front of a bus, was attacked and severely beaten by a bus driver. The case was taken to court.

The driver testified that the foolish man had provoked him. The judge of the Recorder's Court of Montgomery fined the driver $25 and costs and told him that regardless of how the Negro provoked him, he should never have gotten off the bus to beat him.

Another incident occurred when a large Negro woman was boarding through the rear door and the door closed on her, half in, half out. The bus driver hurriedly stopped, opened the door to free her, then collected the names of white witnesses on a slip of paper in case trouble resulted from the incident. Strangely enough, white witnesses could almost always be gotten when, fair or foul, they were needed.

Then there was the mother who boarded the bus with two small babes in her arms. There were no whites on the predominantly Negro bus, so she tenderly placed her two infants on the empty front seat, while she dug into her pocketbook for a dime. The driver demanded in a horrified voice that the "black, dirty brats" instantly be removed from the reserved seat. The alarmed mother dropped her dime into the meter and grabbed for her tiny tots. Not in time, however. For at that same moment, the operator lunged the vehicle forward with a terrific jerk, throwing the two small ones into the aisle.

Sympathetic passengers picked up the howling infants and gave them to the mother, whose face was bathed in tears. In deep humiliation and fear for the physical condition of her children, she got off at the next stop.

There was the old gray-haired driver on the Capitol Heights line, who said to a bus packed with black passengers and two whites that if the whites were not aboard, he would "wreck the god-damn bus and kill all the black sons of bitches."

Another soul-stirring tale circulated that on a freezing day in November, just before the bus protest began, a large crowd of domestic workers boarded the bus for an exclusive section, Cloverdale, where they worked for whites. No whites were aboard that morning. Buses to Cloverdale were usually crowded with these domestic helpers in the early morning and and again in the late afternoon when they came off duty. Meanwhile, whites rode from home into town in the mornings and back again in the afternoon. Thus, black passengers occupied the buses going one way and whites the other.

On this particular morning the bus was filled with black passengers, except, of course, for the ten empty double seats at the front. Icicles hung heavily from limbs of trees and frozen ponds glared in the sunlight. It was one of the coldest mornings Montgomery had that season. One of the domestics informed the operator that the passengers were old and that the bus was cold, and she requested the driver to "turn up the heat" on the bus so that they could get warm. The driver complied with the passenger's request by opening the front and rear doors of the bus for a moment, allowing high winds to blow in, chilling the already cold occupants. All lips clamped shut so no further requests came from the chattering teeth of the passengers as they huddled closer together on the crowded bus, sitting two or three to a seat or standing in the crowded aisle over the ten empty reserved double seats at the front.

The reader must understand, of course, that the bus drivers were charged by their employers with keeping the buses segregated, for segregation was the law of the land in Alabama during this time. Brutality, however, whether physical or mental, was another matter. Not all drivers were guilty of such practices; there were some very fine, courteous bus drivers who were kindly disposed and carried out the laws of segregation without offending the riders. They must not be numbered with those drivers who took delight in humiliating black customers. Some drivers who "knew" their customers from daily contact would stop at bus stops to pick up riders or see persons running to board the bus and wait for them to get on before driving away. Others did not; some drivers closed their doors in the faces of late arrivals hurrying to board the carriers. There were good and mean drivers, considerate and hateful ones. And black bus riders had to cope with both types.

There were literally thousands of times when Negroes were made to stand up over seats "reserved" for whites. In many instances not one white passenger was aboard. In others, perhaps one or two white people occupied seats, keeping the other reserved seats free of black passengers. Yet thirty or forty black riders jammed the aisles where men and women, old and young, mothers with babies in their arms, or women with huge packages, stood swaying or falling over those empty seats, where they dared not sit down.

When and if the first ten double seats were ever taken by the white riders, then black riders who occupied the seats next to them, in the section behind the reserved seats, had to get up if more whites got on. Old black men and women were even forced to get out of seats so that white school children could sit down.

The practice of "reserved seats" had become an ultimate humiliation. The ten empty seats became an obsession to weary workers, whose tired feet and aching backs urged them to sit down. The number *ten* became a damnable number. Whether the number *ten* referred to the ten reserved seats on the bus, or the number of a theater ticket, or a tag number, it signified bad luck. Nobody wanted that number on anything that belonged to him. It loomed large, formidable. It was actually a mental, a psychological omen: Threatening! Deadly!

Some operators snatched transfers from the hands of black passengers, or threw transfers or change in coins at them. Some drivers refused to make change for Negroes and accepted only exact fares from them. Today, to reduce risk of theft, most transit lines make no change, and *all* passengers must have correct change. But back in 1955, in small cities like Montgomery, drivers could and did make change for riders—if they chose to do so, that is.

However, if the black rider had no change, he was put off the bus and made to walk, unless other passengers could make change for him. Sometimes passengers who wanted transfers had to stand waiting as the driver drove for one or two blocks before throwing the slips of paper at them. The humble ones bent down and picked them up from the floor and said nothing. Those less restrained, retaliated in bitter, inaudible tones. Nevertheless, if they wanted the despicable pieces of paper, they, too, bent and picked them up.

On rainy days black riders were "passed by" by some of the "yellow monsters," as the buses had come to be called. "Wet, bulksome, and smelly," as the drivers described blacks, whites did not want them standing over them, or "passing by them" on their way to the back. Thus, drivers often drove past them without stopping on rainy days, leaving them standing there to wait for the next bus, or the next, or the next. Those waiting could either continue to wait in the rain or cold for the next bus, or walk to work or home.

Black riders would often forget pride and feeling, forget the terribly offensive names they were so often called when they dared to sit in one of the ten reserved seats. Hurting feet, tired bodies, empty stomachs often tempted them to sit down. Names like "black nigger," "black bitches," "heifers," "whores," and so on, brought them to their feet again. When sheer exhaustion or tired, aching limbs forced them to forget pride and feeling, they sat down, sometimes for one minute, maybe two. Even a minute's rest helped some. But they would rise again, either in tears, or retaliating curses hurled by them at the driver. Whatever the case was, they would be badly shaken, nervous, tired, fearful, and angry.

Scholars have attempted to explain what effects such attacks upon the human nervous system could have days afterward on individual conduct. Bus incidents could often lead to domestic trouble in Negro families, or to juvenile delinquency, which had been on the rise among Montgomery's black children for some time. Even adult delinquency and crime have been attributed to similar situations, as sheer exasperation in one instance later led to needless suffering or even death in another. This was too often the case.

The Women's Political Council, over a long period, tried to ascertain why there was so much killing, cutting, intoxication, and burglary, etc., on weekends among black children and adults. We discovered that all the pent-up emotions resulting from bitter experiences on local transportation lines often were released upon husbands, wives, or children, resulting in injuries that necessitated hospital care.

Grown men frequently came home on particular evenings, angry from humiliating experiences on buses, to pick fights with their wives or children. They needed a target somewhere, a way to relieve internal conflict. These quarrels often ended in cuttings or killings, divorce or separation. When these men were later approached in a kind, understanding manner by some WPC member and asked why such crimes had occurred, these grown men—hard, tough and penitent—would cry with body-shaking sobs as they tried to explain, without really knowing why, what had made them do such things. If women were involved, they gave their children unnecessary beatings. Children, imitating the adults in their lives, resentfully fought other children, robbed stores or houses, stole bicycles, or played hooky from school. They often beat their pets severely for no apparent reason.

In 1956, the superintendent of a local hospital, which customarily treated many weekend fight victims, told a reporter that since the boycott began, the hospital had had fewer such patients. Thus the hospital official corroborated the WPC's findings that bitter bus experiences could have caused, or greatly contributed to, serious weekend fights in the home. After December 5, 1955, the people were able to release their suppressed emotions through the boycott movement, which allowed them to retaliate directly for the pain, humiliation, and embarrassment they had endured over the years at the hands of drivers and policemen while riding on the buses. And there was no need for family fights and weekend brawls.

The number of Negro men walking increased during 1954 and early 1955. They walked to and from work, to town, to movies, to see their girlfriends, because of fear of riding the buses. At no time did a single man ever stand up in defense of the women. Although it hurt to be called "coward," perhaps they were cowards, except for a very few men who challenged authority and paid the price. For, at the first hint of conflict, the men left at the nearest exit. They didn't dare to challenge the bus operators, who possessed police powers. The men feared arrest and did not expect to get justice in the courts. They had wives and children and could not afford to lose their jobs or to go to jail. If they were on the bus when trouble started, they merely got up and got off. Or they avoided getting on the bus in the first place. They rode when forced to, walked when they did not get rides or could not afford taxi fare. But they were tired, and they murmured!

Then came the day when Claudette Colvin was arrested. She was a fifteen-year-old student at Booker Washington High School— an "A" student, quiet, well-mannered, neat, clean, intelligent, pretty, and deeply religious.

On March 2, 1955, Claudette got on the bus and sat, not in the first ten reserved seats, but two seats from the rear door of the bus. Black and white riders crowded in, and soon no more seats were available. The aisle was jammed with passengers standing—many blacks, a few whites. The driver stopped the vehicle and demanded that blacks get up who were seated in rows not normally reserved for whites, those behind the first ten double seats. At first no one moved, for there was nowhere to move to. The aisle was crowded with whites and blacks. No seat was available.

The demand was repeated. Negro men sensed trouble. With their heavy responsibilities at home, they could ill afford arrest. The apprehensive ones got off the bus and walked away. Slowly but surely, Negroes who had been seated stood up. Whites sat in the vacated seats. Finally, the driver stood over Claudette and demanded that she relinquish her seat to a white person.

By now, the remaining standing black men had gotten off the bus and left the scene. The aisle was practically clear, except for a few whites waiting to take seats as they were made available.

Claudette looked around and saw no empty seat. She knew she was not in the restricted area, the first ten. She knew, too, that she was far enough back to be entitled to her seat. So, without any trepidation, she remained seated.

A pregnant Negro woman sat next to Claudette. At the driver's insistence she got up and stood in the aisle. A Negro man on the very last seat of the bus gave the pregnant woman his seat and then left the bus. This left Claudette occupying a double seat, alone. Still she did not move. None of the women standing sat down in the one empty seat beside her.

The driver, beside himself with rage by now, drove to town without stopping and called for a street policeman to make the arrest. The policeman came and then another. Obeying the driver's demand that Claudette be arrested, the officers commanded the girl to get up. When she refused, they dragged her, kicking and screaming hysterically, off the bus. Still half-dragging, half-pushing, they forced her into a patrol car which had been summoned, put handcuffs on her wrists so she could do no physical harm to the arresting police, and drove her to jail. There she was charged with misconduct, resisting arrest, and violating the city segregation laws. She remained in jail until bailed out by her pastor.

The news traveled fast. In a few hours every Negro youngster on the streets discussed Claudette's arrest. Telephones rang. Clubs called special meetings and discussed the event with some degree of alarm. Mothers expressed concern about permitting their children on the buses. Men instructed their wives to walk or to share rides in neighbors' autos.

The question of boycotting came up again and loomed in the minds of thousands of black people. We could see that black people— men, women, and children—were tired. The women intuited danger in their men's tiredness, in the limits of their children's and their own endurance. The women felt not that their cup of tolerance was overflowing, but that it had overflowed; they simply could not take anymore. They were ready to boycott. On paper, the WPC had already planned for fifty thousand notices calling people to boycott the buses; only the specifics of time and place had to be added. And, as tempers flared and emotions ran high, the women became active.

But some members were doubtful; some wanted to wait. The women wanted to be certain the entire city was behind them, and opinions differed where Claudette was concerned. Some felt she was too young to be the trigger that precipitated the movement. She might get hurt! The time for action was not now. Not everybody was ready. So, after getting opinions from various groups, the boycott was postponed.

There were some sixty-eight Negro organizations in Montgomery—men's groups, women's groups, and political, religious, social, economic, educational, fraternal, and labor organizations. In the various groups were lawyers, doctors, educators, druggists, entertainers, musicians, farmers, builders, mechanics, maids, cooks, and so on. These organizations touched the total black population, male and female, young people, middle-aged, and old. All such organizations were in existence, yet we were not ready. Nobody came forth with a "time-to-act" suggestion. People had everything to lose and nothing to gain, some of them felt. And "fighting City Hall" was a task nobody had done before, especially fighting to integrate city transportation lines.

It must be understood, too, that most of the people at Alabama State College lived in Montgomery. Their positions were oriented toward Montgomery and sustained by Montgomery. The city was their home, the place of their hopes and dreams, their future. Despite the fact that black citizens of Alabama loved their city, they abhorred the discrimination imposed upon them. They did not want to destroy their city, but to wipe out segregation before it destroyed their race. Thus, they supported any and all movements to destroy the evils of segregation and discrimination. But many of them took no overt role themselves. We have seen how Dr. Mary Fair Burks organized the WPC to fight segregation. Dr. Martin Luther King and the ministers, along with Mr. E. D. Nixon, Mr. Rufus Lewis, and many others, established the Montgomery Improvement Association. But they did not call the boycott.

Thus, a period of unrest began that permeated the thoughts of blacks. During this period the presidents of all the clubs of the city formed one large body to represent their organizations. At the first meeting this coordination committee, composed of two representatives of each organization, was created. Mr. Rufus Lewis was elected president. Other offices were claimed by some of the top educators of the city. Despite the fact that the Lewises and some of the other members of the group were self-employed and financially secure, nobody had called for the boycott! Black Americans were still riding those buses, and still being insulted as they rode. Black leaders were still trying to compromise with officials for better treatment, and still enduring embarrassing experiences each day.

Additionally, the ministers met regularly under the aegis of the Interdenominational Ministerial Alliance. That group included all the black ministers in the community. The ministers met weekly at various churches, just to get together, to sing and pray, and to keep up with the turn of events. They would be "serving the Lord" but learning politics too.

Taking the same intelligent approach, this coordination committee named a special committee to join others in consulting with Commissioner Dave Birmingham, who had jurisdiction over the police force. Representatives from churches and special organizations, ministers, businessmen, one physician, a number of women including myself, and several other teachers who got permission to attend went to the meeting. The other two commissioners were nearby throughout the session and occasionally entered for a few moments.

Commissioner Birmingham received us and heard our protest. A gentleman, an honest man, and a Christian, Mr. Birmingham had won election as commissioner on the basis of his integrity, honesty, and fairmindedness. He would listen, question, and attempt to correct the problem.

He immediately arranged for a meeting with the policemen who had arrested Claudette, the bus company officials, and the bus driver who had requested the arrest of the girl.

In that meeting the police officers admitted that, in arresting the girl, they had acted under the command of the driver. Mr. J. H. Bagley, the bus company manager, spoke for the driver, who, though he had been requested to be present, did not attend the meeting. Bagley stated that the driver had admitted to him that the girl had been sitting in the back and that there were no other seats available at the time.

Those at the hearing were given to understand by Commissioner Birmingham that justice would be extended in this case and that Claudette would be given every fair chance to clear her name. It was not a trial to determine guilt or innocence, but an effort to find out the truth, and, if the girl were found innocent, her record would be clear.

Those present left the conference feeling that we had acted wisely in not calling a boycott, and that everything would work out fairly for everyone. Following this meeting, and to minimize such incidents on public conveyances, city lawyers, bus company lawyers, and black lawyers promised to confer on redefining the law affecting transit lines, so that all would know what the law meant for everyone. As far as I know, this never took place.

However, the meeting had served a good purpose, and those attending felt that Commissioner Birmingham was an honest man who showed concern for human personality; that he had tried to answer questions and to explain the laws that governed city transportation; and that he had shown his concern for those customers who had been arrested on city transportation lines because of the color of their skin. But these qualities may have cost him re-election in the next race, which took place in March 1955. Forced into a runoff, he announced that his "health forced him to withdraw from the race" before the runoff took place. Commissioner Clyde Sellers took over the police department, and Frank Parks was elected to the third seat in place of George Cleere.

Claudette Colvin's case came up, but instead of being tried under the city law, under which she was arrested and booked, she was tried under state law. (While the city ordinance provided that no one could be convicted of failing to vacate a seat unless another seat was available for that person, the state law contained no such requirement, and simply gave drivers the legal authority to assign seats as they chose.)

Instead of being exonerated as we anticipated, Claudette Colvin was found guilty and released on indefinite probation in her parents' care. She had remained calm all during the days of her waiting period and during the trial, but when she was found guilty, Claudette's agonized sobs penetrated the atmosphere of the court-house. Many people brushed away their own tears.

The verdict was a bombshell! Blacks were as near a breaking point as they had ever been. Resentment, rebellion, and unrest were evident in all Negro circles. For a few days, large numbers refused to use the buses, but as they cooled off somewhat, they gradually drifted back. Cold weather and rain, too, encouraged a return to the buses. But there was much discontented grumbling; complaints streamed in from everywhere to attest to people's resentment.

The public reaction was sympathetic to Claudette. Many black and white people contributed money to help with her case, which was appealed to a higher court. White people as far away as California and Oregon sent money to help pay legal fees. Hundreds of expressions of support from people throughout the country encouraged her and boosted her morale.

She needed the encouragement, for since her conviction as a law violator, her head was not held so high. She did not look people straight in the eye as before. Her classmates stared at her, and curiosity-seekers made a special effort to see "the girl who had been arrested." Claudette, who had never sought notoriety, could not understand laws that did such terrible things to people. She still does not understand.

Following this event, other complaints poured in. It was useless to complain to the bus company or to the City Commission. They totally ignored all complaints. The plight of the black bus riders was insupportable, and matters were gradually becoming worse.

In October 1955, Mary Louise Smith, an eighteen-year-old black girl, was arrested and fined for refusing to move to the rear of the bus. Her case was unpublicized and no one knew about it until after her arrest and conviction. She, too, was found guilty; she paid her fine and kept on riding the bus.

Intermittently, twenty to twenty-five thousand black people in Montgomery rode city buses, and I would estimate that, up until the boycott of December 5, 1955, about three out of five had suffered some unhappy experience on the public transit lines. But the straw that broke the camel's back came on Thursday, December 1, 1955, when an incident occurred which was almost a repeat performance of the Claudette Colvin case.

In the afternoon of Thursday, December 1, a prominent black woman named Mrs. Rosa Parks was arrested for refusing to vacate her seat for a white man. Mrs. Parks was a medium-sized, cultured mulatto woman; a civic and religious worker; quiet, unassuming, and pleasant in manner and appearance; dignified and reserved; of high morals and a strong character. She was—and still is, for she lives to tell the story—respected in all black circles. By trade she was a seamstress, adept and competent in her work.

Tired from work, Mrs. Parks boarded a bus. The "reserved seats" were partially filled, but the seats just behind the reserved section were vacant, and Mrs. Parks sat down in one. It was during the busy evening rush hour. More black and white passengers boarded the bus, and soon all the reserved seats were occupied. The driver demanded that Mrs. Parks get up and surrender her seat to a white man, but she was tired from her work. Besides, she was a woman, and the person waiting was a man. She remained seated.

In a few minutes, police summoned by the driver appeared, placed Mrs. Parks under arrest, and took her to jail.

It was the first time the soft-spoken, middle-aged woman had been arrested. She maintained decorum and poise, and the word of her arrest spread. Mr. E. D. Nixon, a longtime stalwart of our NAACP branch, along with liberal white attorney Clifford Durr and his wife Virginia, went to the jail and obtained Mrs. Parks's release on bond. Her trial was scheduled for Monday, December 5, 1955.

The news traveled like wildfire into every black home. Telephones jangled; people congregated on street corners and in homes and talked. But nothing was done. A numbing helplessness seemed to paralyze everyone. Very few stayed off the buses the rest of that day or the next. There was fear, discontent, and uncertainty. Everyone seemed to wait for someone to *do* something, but nobody made a move. For that day and a half, black Americans rode the buses as before, as if nothing had happened. They were sullen and uncommunicative, but they rode the buses. There was a silent, tension-filled waiting. For blacks were not talking loudly in public places—they were quiet, sullen, waiting. Just waiting!

Thursday evening came and went. Thursday night was far spent, when, at about 11:30 P.M., I sat alone in my peaceful single-family dwelling on a quiet street. I was thinking about the situation. Lost in thought, I was startled by the telephone's ring. Black attorney Fred Gray, who had been out of town all day, had just gotten back and was returning the phone message I had left for him about Mrs. Parks's arrest. Attorney Gray, though a very young man, had been one of my most active colleagues in our previous meetings with bus company officials and Commissioner Birmingham. A Montgomery native who had attended Alabama State and been one of my students, Fred Gray had gone on to law school in Ohio before returning to his home town to open a practice with the only other black lawyer in Montgomery, Charles Langford.

Fred Gray and his wife Bernice were good friends of mine, and we talked often. In addition to being a lawyer, Gray was a trained, ordained minister of the gospel, actively serving as assistant pastor of Holt Street Church of Christ.

Tonight his voice on the phone was very short and to the point. Fred was shocked by the news of Mrs. Parks's arrest. I informed him that I already was thinking that the WPC should distribute thousands of notices calling for all bus riders to stay off the buses on Monday, the day of Mrs. Parks's trial. "Are you ready?," he asked. Without hesitation, I assured him that we were. With that he hung up, and I went to work.

I made some notes on the back of an envelope: "The Women's Political Council will not wait for Mrs. Parks's consent to call for a boycott of city buses. On Friday, December 2, 1955, the women of Montgomery will call for a boycott to take place on Monday, December 5."

Some of the WPC officers previously had discussed plans for distributing thousands of notices announcing a bus boycott. Now the time had come for me to write just such a notice. I sat down and quickly drafted a message and then called a good friend and colleague, John Cannon, chairman of the business department at the college, who had access to the college's mimeograph equipment. When I told him that the WPC was staging a boycott and needed to run off the notices, he told me that he too had suffered embarrassment on the city buses. Like myself, he had been hurt and angry. He said that he would happily assist me. Along with two of my most trusted senior students, we quickly agreed to meet almost immediately, in the middle of the night, at the college's duplicating room. We were able to get three messages to a page, greatly reducing the number of pages that had to be mimeographed in order to produce the tens of thousands of leaflets we knew would be needed. By 4 A.M. Friday, the sheets had been duplicated, cut in thirds, and bundled. Each leaflet read:

> Another Negro woman has been arrested and thrown in jail because she refused to get up out of her seat on the bus for a white person to sit down. It is the second time since the Claudette Colvin case that a Negro woman has been arrested for the same thing. This has to be stopped. Negroes have rights, too, for if Negroes did not ride the buses, they could not operate. Three-fourths of the riders are Negroes, yet we are arrested, or have to stand over empty seats. If we do not do something to stop these arrests, they will continue.

The next time it may be you, or your daughter, or mother. This woman's case will come up on Monday. We are, therefore, asking every Negro to stay off the buses Monday in protest of the arrest and trial. Don't ride the buses to work, to town, to school, or anywhere on Monday. You can afford to stay out of school for one day if you have no other way to go except by bus. You can also afford to stay out of town for one day. If you work, take a cab, or walk. But please, children and grown-ups, don't ride the bus at all on Monday. Please stay off of all buses Monday.

Between 4 and 7 A.M., the two students and I mapped out distribution routes for the notices. Some of the WPC officers previously had discussed how and where to deliver thousands of leaflets announcing a boycott, and those plans now stood me in good stead. We outlined our routes, arranged the bundles in sequences, stacked them in our cars, and arrived at my 8 A.M. class, in which both young men were enrolled, with several minutes to spare. We weren't even tired or hungry. Just like me, the two students felt a tremendous sense of satisfaction at being able to contribute to the cause of justice.

After class my two students and I quickly finalized our plans for distributing the thousands of leaflets so that one would reach every black home in Montgomery. I took out the WPC membership roster and called the former president, Dr. Mary Fair Burks, then the Pierces, the Glasses, Mrs. Mary Cross, Mrs. Elizabeth Arrington, Mrs. Josie Lawrence, Mrs. Geraldine Nesbitt, Mrs. H. Councill Trenholm, Mrs. Catherine N. Johnson, and a dozen or more others. I alerted all of them to the forthcoming distribution of the leaflets, and enlisted their aid in speeding and organizing the distribution network. Each would have one person waiting at a certain place to take a package of notices as soon as my car stopped and the young men could hand them a bundle of leaflets.

Then I and my two student helpers set out. Throughout the late morning and early afternoon hours we dropped off tens of thousands of leaflets. Some of our bundles were dropped off at schools, where both students and staff members helped distribute them further and spread the word for people to read the notices and then pass them on to neighbors. Leaflets were also dropped off at business places, storefronts, beauty parlors, beer halls, factories, barber shops, and every other available place. Workers would pass along notices both to other employees as well as to customers.

During those hours of crucial work, nothing went wrong. Suspicion was never raised. The action of all involved was so casual, so unconcerned, so nonchalant, that suspicion was never raised, and neither the city nor its people ever suspected a thing! We never missed a spot. And no one missed a class, a job, or a normal routine. Everything was done by the plan, with perfect timing. By 2 o'clock, thousands of the mimeographed handbills had changed hands many times. Practically every black man, woman, and child in Montgomery knew the plan and was passing the word along. No one knew where the notices had come from or who had arranged for their circulation, and no one cared. Those who passed them on did so efficiently, quietly, and without comment. But deep within the heart of every black person was a joy he or she dared not reveal.

Meanwhile, at the college, one of the women teachers who was not a member of the Women's Political Council, nor even a resident of Montgomery (she lived in Mobile), took a leaflet as I and my two seniors got into my car to leave the campus on our delivery route. She carried that leaflet straight to the office of the president of Alabama State College, Dr. H. Councill Trenholm.

Dr. Trenholm was president of Alabama State College for a total of thirty-eight years. When I first came to teach at ASC, a number of long-time teachers there told me that when Dr. Trenholm became president of ASC, following in the footsteps of his father, H. Councill Trenholm, Sr., who had been president for five years before him, he was a young man, brilliant, easy-going, and friendly with his colleagues, many of whom were twice or more his age. He made them feel comfortable during individual conference periods. Even when he criticized or found fault with a teacher's work, what he said was more of a suggestion or recommendation for a better method than a blunt criticism. And nobody but the two of them, he and that teacher, ever knew what the conference was all about. The teachers loved him for that!

He was a diligent worker, a stickler for perfection—a "work ox," somebody labeled him. The institution was a junior college when he first took over, with a few students, limited grounds, and even fewer teachers. He immediately began to go out, meet people, introduce himself, and give scholarships to the very poor and deserving students who wanted to go on but had no money to matriculate. Being a young, ambitious man, he began visiting the immediate communities and talking with parents and young people who were hoping for a college education. In a very short time, he had a large number of students matriculating. He was in a tough position because state funds for "black" college students were limited, and in some places there was no appropriation at all for black students. However, Dr. Trenholm talked with state officials, plus local financiers, and things began to change. Enrollments increased; parents became involved. The junior college became a senior college, and seniors graduated. The state purchased more land, added more space, and the student body grew.

During the Depression, when funds were limited, Dr. Trenholm had helped fund the institution with money from his own savings and from money-raising projects. He gave his youth, his intellect, his *all* to ASC. In so doing, he built an institution that was an intellectual light to the city of Montgomery and the state of Alabama. Thousands of graduates are rendering service to mankind all over the United States and even in other parts of the globe.

When I returned to the campus that Friday for my two o'clock class, after delivering the notices, I found a message from Dr. Trenholm, asking me to come to his office immediately. Very angry and visibly shaken, the president showed me the leaflet and demanded to know what the movement was about and what *my* role was. I informed Dr. Trenholm of the arrest of Mrs. Rosa Parks and of how in the past others had been arrested for the same thing, for refusing to give up their seats to white people.

"Were there other seats?" he asked. I assured him there were not. I informed him that there were many adults who had been arrested for the same thing, and that because the college had no direct connection with the persons, college personnel often had no way of knowing about it. I stressed the fact that black people, innocent black people young and old, were suffering, and that they could not help themselves.

"What are they being arrested for?" he asked. And I did not hesitate to inform him. For all of a sudden, I remembered that time when I was made to get up from a seat in the fifth row from the front of a bus, when there were only three people riding the entire bus.

"I have sent for a teacher; she will be here soon to take charge of your class," he said, in a voice which was not conciliatory. "Sit down and tell me about this situation."

In this powerful man's presence I felt fear for the first time, a fear that penetrated my entire being. He had a frown on his face; his voice revealed impatience. For the first time I felt that he might fire me. But at that moment, I did not care if he did! I breathed a silent prayer for guidance and felt a wave of peace inundate me. I knew then that if he fired me, I would stay right there until the fight was won.

I described the frequent repetition of these outrages, how many children, men, and women, old and middle-aged people, had been humiliated and made to relinquish their seats to white people. I told him of Claudette Colvin and of Mrs. Rosa Parks, both of whom had been jailed. He stopped me several times to ask questions; then I would proceed.

As I talked, I could see the anger slowly receding from his face and heard his tone of voice softening. Concern began to show in his expression, as he settled in his chair. I relaxed a bit. Then I told him of the three hundred black women who had organized the WPC to fight any inhumane impositions upon black people. I assured him that the WPC would never involve the college, that ASC had not been mentioned nor would it ever be. I convinced him also that if some intelligent, organized group did not take the initiative and seek improvements from the city hall power structure, angry hot-heads would resort to other means. We would choose to fight not with weapons, but with reason. When I told him that somebody, or some organization, had to fight this assault on blacks' rights, and that the WPC was prepared to do it, I felt that I had said enough. I sat with my eyes cast downward breathing a prayer while I waited for his response. His anger gone, deep sympathetic concern spread over his face; his eyes seemed to penetrate the walls of his office; he sat for a moment, pondering, lost in thought. He seemed to have aged years in the brief span of our conversation, and he leaned on his desk as he talked to me. He seemed so tired.

Then he said: "Your group must continue to press for civil rights." He cautioned me, however, to be careful, to work behind the scenes, not to involve the college, and not to neglect my responsibilities as a member of the faculty of Alabama State College. Then he stood up to indicate the discussion was ended.

After thanking him for his understanding and encouragement, I hurried toward the outer door of his office, filled with happiness that he had understood and given us his support. My talk with him had been a wonderful experience.

But before the door closed completely, he called me back.

"Jo Ann," he said, smiling now.

"Yes, Dr. Trenholm?" I responded hesitatingly, realizing he had not yet finished.

"I called Mr. John Cannon's office after receiving this notice of the boycott. Mr. Cannon confirmed my suspicion that you ran off these boycott notices on school paper."

"Yes, sir, that is correct," I admitted. "Let me see, sir. We used thirty-five reams of paper at 500 sheets per ream. That made 17,500 sheets, cut into thirds, for a total of 52,500 leaflets distributed. So by my count, sir, the Women's Political Council owes Mr. Cannon's office for thirty-five reams of paper. We will find out the cost from Mr. Cannon and pay that bill immediately, sir." Actually, the WPC *had no treasury!* I paid that bill out of my own pocket.

As we will see, once the battle was begun, the bus company and city officials would request Dr. Trenholm to sit on a board with them to help arrive at a satisfactory conclusion of the boycott.

Dr. Trenholm did not participate personally in the boycott. But he was mentally and spiritually involved—and deeply so! He was financially involved, too, and often contributed to the collections for people who were suffering because of the loss of their jobs. He never went onto the housetop and screamed of what his contributions had been, but his actions, his constant advice, his donations, and his guidance amounted to much more than dollars and cents.

Dr. Trenholm's wife, Portia, was a brilliant, talented, highly-trained lady, an accomplished pianist who taught music at ASC. She and I were good friends. Although Portia was not a member of the WPC or, later, the Montgomery Improvement Association, she played a key role in the bus boycott ordeal. Like all faculty members at the college, she gave rides to pedestrians during her free periods between classes and contributed funds to help keep the station wagons in operation. She was just as sympathetic to the boycott cause as the rest of the faculty. But most important, she was my "information passport" to Dr. Trenholm's office, day or night, early or late. I had promised Dr. Trenholm that I would "keep him informed," and with Portia's help I kept that promise throughout the boycott. He knew in advance what the WPC's plans were; he neither advised nor protested the plans. Many people sympathized with the president and his wife and kept them informed. Because Portia relayed the messages to her husband, Dr. Trenholm knew more of the facts of the boycott than many of those who were "walking for the cause."

I could not just telephone Dr. Trenholm's office and talk to him directly. According to the protocol of the black intellectual arena, faculty members respect their leaders. And when I had, of necessity, to consult with Dr. Trenholm at night about the boycott, a matter which was practically alien to the college jurisdiction, I could not simply call him at his office. I called his home, and talked with his wife first. She would buzz him to see if he could speak with me, and then I would be connected. Or if he was busy, I talked with her. I explained to her everything I wanted conveyed to him, and she would relay the message when he was in a position to receive it.

I called Portia each night to report the progress made on bus authorities' attitude or other facts. She could get ideas from Dr. Trenholm, who was a brilliant man, and she would pass them along to me; I in turn would relay them to the relevant organization, which would carry on from there. No matter the hour, if the WPC needed advice, I as president would call Portia, and she would relay the message to Dr. Trenholm and give me his answer. Many times I went to him for advice for the WPC, and he never sent me away without submitting workable solutions to almost insoluble problems. Each answer he gave took consideration of the students, the college, and the masses who walked the streets daily for a better way of life, for he loved them all. His answers were in line with those of the ministers, for all we were demanding was justice on the buses. The Trenholms' concern reached out to the entire body of teachers, students, workers, and all that touched the college family. They were involved!

Thus I worked on the boycott with Dr. Trenholm's approval. Even so, I never missed a class! Or if I did, I made up the time. It wasn't easy. I had ten minutes' break to change classes, a thirty-minute morning break, forty-five minutes for lunch, and then back to class for the rest of the day. All crucial meetings pertaining to the boycott were scheduled during my off periods, evenings, and Saturdays. Nobody complained. But if I had to leave a class, I gave the students work to do, for I never, in thirty years of teaching, went to a class without a lesson plan. I worked and got paid for my service, both in terms of finance and students' gratitude. Students knew that I was asked to serve, and they were proud, for they would have an opportunity to speak their opinion, and they had excellent ideas. I taught white and black students and never saw color. I was pleased that I had such support for my involvement in the planning and subsequent day-to-day activities of the Montgomery Bus Boycott.

2

The Boycott Begins

On Friday morning, December 2, 1955, a goodly number of Montgomery's black clergymen happened to be meeting at the Hilliard Chapel A.M.E. Zion Church on Highland Avenue. When the Women's Political Council officers learned that the ministers were assembled in that meeting, we felt that God was on our side. It was easy for my two students and me to leave a handful of our circulars at the church, and those disciples of God could not truthfully have told where the notices came from if their very lives had depended on it. Many of the ministers received their notices of the boycott at the same time, in the same place. They all felt equal, included, appreciated, needed. It seemed predestined that this should be so.

One minister read the circular, inquired about the announcements, and found that all the city's black congregations were quite intelligent on the matter and were planning to support the one-day boycott with or without their ministers' leadership. It was then that the ministers decided that it was time for them, the leaders, to catch up with the masses. If the people were really determined to stage this one-day protest, then they would need moral support and Christian leadership. The churches could serve as channels of communication, as well as altars where people could come for prayer and spiritual guidance. Since the ministers were servants of the people and of God, and believed in the gospel of social justice, and since the churches were institutions supported by the people, the clerics could serve as channels through which all the necessary benefits could flow. Thus, for the first time in the history of Montgomery, black ministers united to lead action for civic improvement. There was no thought of denomination. Baptists, Presbyterians, Episcopalians, Lutherans, Congregationalists, and others joined together and became one band of ministerial brothers, offering their leadership to the masses. Had they not done so, they might have alienated themselves from their congregations and indeed lost members, for the masses were ready, and they were united!

The black ministers and their churches made the Montgomery Bus Boycott of 1955–1956 the success that it was. Had it not been for the ministers and the support they received from their wonderful congregations, the outcome of the boycott might have been different. The ministers gave themselves, their time, their contributions, their minds, their prayers, and their leadership, all of which set examples for the laymen to follow. They gave us confidence, faith in ourselves, faith in them and their leadership, that helped the congregations to support the movement every foot of the way.

Under the aegis of the Interdenominational Ministerial Alliance a meeting was called for that Friday evening at the Dexter Avenue Baptist Church, of which the Reverend Dr. Martin Luther King, Jr., was pastor. To this meeting were invited all the ministers, all club presidents and officers, all church organization heads, and any interested persons.

In the meantime, domestic workers who worked late into the day toyed with the slips of paper carrying the important information of the protest. Most of them destroyed the evidence, buried the information in their memories, and went merrily on their way to work. However, one lone black woman, a domestic loyal to her "white lady," in spite of her concern over the plight of her black peers and without any sense of obligation to her people, carried the handbill to her job and did not stop until the precious paper was safe in her "white lady's" hands. It was only a matter of minutes before the bus company, the City Commission, the chief of police, and the press knew its contents. The *Alabama Journal,* Montgomery's afternoon newspaper, ran a story on Saturday. Another article appeared in the

Montgomery Advertiser on Sunday. The two local television stations and the four radio stations completed the coverage. The secret was out.

In recalling this particular incident later, the leaders of the boycott wondered if that woman's action had been providential, part of a divine plan to make the boycott succeed. If this was the case, she was not disloyal to her people, but rather was following the dictates of a higher authority!

The original intention had been that the whole affair would come as a complete surprise to whites. Then if all the darker set did not cooperate, no one would be the wiser. But now the news was out, and some misgivings and fear among blacks followed. Southern blacks, who had never been known to stick together as a group, to follow leadership, or to keep their mouths shut from exposing secrets, were on the spot!

One good thing, however, came from the revelation: the few black citizens in remote corners of the city who might not have gotten the news of the boycott, knew it now. The news that circulated through the newspapers, radio, television, and other channels of communication covered every possible isolated place not reached by the leaflets.

Publicity given the Monday boycott probably accounted, too, for the very large attendance which turned out for the Friday night meeting at Dexter Avenue Baptist Church. More than one hundred leaders were present.

There the organization of the boycott began. Special committees were set up. The main one focused on transportation. To help the walking public, volunteer cars had to be pooled, taxis had to be contacted, and donations had to be determined through cooperative means. Routes had to be mapped out to get workers to all parts of the city. Regular bus routes had to be followed so that workers who "walked along" the streets could be picked up. This committee, headed by Alfonso Campbell and staffed by volunteer workers, worked all night Friday to complete this phase of the program. The pickup system was so effectively planned that many writers described it as comparable in precision to a military operation.

What the ministers failed to do at that meeting was to select one person who would head the boycott. Those present discussed it, pointing out the leadership preparation of various individuals, but no definite decision was made. That had to wait until Monday afternoon, when the ministers realized that the one-day boycott was going to be successful. Then they met again, and Dr. Martin Luther King, Jr., agreed to accept the leadership post.

On Friday night the group at Dexter Avenue did decide to arrange a mass meeting for Monday night following the one-day boycott. Holt Street Baptist Church, of which Reverend A. W. Wilson was pastor, was chosen as the place for the Monday night meeting because it was the most spacious of all Montgomery's Negro churches. It had a large basement that accommodated hundreds, an even larger main auditorium, and an upstairs area as well. In addition, various smaller rooms were equipped with loudspeakers. Thus, thousands could fit within this one building. And around the building was a huge outdoor space which seemed to cover several acres. Outside loudspeakers would be able to carry the message to those who could not squeeze into the church.

The Monday evening rally was planned in an effort to calm emotions and to keep the infuriated masses under control. Every citizen knew that, as tense as people were over the situation, violence could break out among those individuals, white or black, whose emotions were not well-disciplined. From this standpoint it was good, too, that the ministers had agreed to take over the boycott's leadership, to direct an emotional appeal for passive resistance.

A second purpose of the Monday night meeting was to get a clear report of the effectiveness of the boycott that day, for decisions would have to be made. The meeting could help determine whether the boycott should continue and establish definite plans if it were to continue.

The WPC prepared notices of this Monday night meeting, which were carried by diligent community workers from door to door, as the first ones had been, until they were circulated over the city. One of these flyers, too, fell into the hands of the press. Unknowingly, the journalists helped our group considerably by publicizing the mass meeting for Monday night, and, by playing up the expression "further instructions," they aroused the interest of blacks and whites alike and heightened concern at the Montgomery City Lines.

As was customary, on the dot of the hour Monday morning, December 5, 1955, empty buses lumbered out of the Montgomery City Lines car shed, and drove off in all directions to begin their daily rounds. Trailing each bus were two motorcycle policemen, who had been assigned to follow each bus into predominantly black population areas to "protect Negro riders" who would want to patronize the city transportation lines. Rumors had spread that hundreds of black domestics had telephoned their "white folks" that they would not be at work on Monday because they were "afraid to ride the bus." This was interpreted to mean that other Negroes would try to keep them from boarding the public conveyances by doing them bodily harm. So local authorities increased the police force with extras, and posted two officers on the tail of every bus that went into neighborhoods inhabited mainly by the minority group. This extra protection presumably would enable maids and cooks to go to work without fear of their own boycotting people.

The headlines in the city's morning newspapers were bold and glaring. The *Montgomery Adviser* carried the caption: "Extra Police Set for Patrol Work in Trolley Boycott." The article stated that "Negro goon squads" reportedly had been organized to intimidate other Negroes who rode buses on Monday, and that the threat was being met by city authorities with the promise to "call out every city policeman and every reserve policeman, if necessary, to maintain law and order." Officials had referred to the boycott as a "most serious matter," which would be dealt with accordingly. Further, the article stated, black domestics had telephoned their employers that they would not show up for work that day unless the employers came for them in their automobiles or paid their taxi fares.

Boycotters had not heard of any "goon squads." Since they knew that the boycott was a purely voluntary gesture which thousands of blacks heartily approved of and encouraged, they failed to believe the report. The news was ignored or scoffed at.

The news did one thing, however. If there were any timid souls who would have ridden the bus despite the boycott, they were really frightened now. Hence the media assisted the boycott's leaders in preventing would-be-riders from boarding buses.

Early Monday the first buses went out for the regular morning's pickup. Usually at this time people pushed on or scrambled for seats. But today no passengers awaited the buses' arrival. It was reported that at the very beginning a few riders were spotted on several of the buses. There were in fact a few blacks who had threatened to ignore requests to stay off buses that day. These had been well-indoctrinated into believing that white people were superior, and that blacks had "their place" and should stay in it. But fate seemed to play into the hands of the boycotters. When these faint-hearted few saw the two motorcycle police escorts accompanying the buses, they became really frightened that they might be arrested if they rode the bus. So they took a cab for a dime instead. (The cabs were provided by black citizens cooperating with the group.) Soon, on most of the public carriers, there was "nary a colored soul to pay a single fare." Instead, hundreds of people were walking or boarding taxis or private cars.

There were no black late-risers on this particular morning, for those who lived on bus lines telephoned those who did not, to say that the boycott was effective, that black passengers were not riding, and that very few whites were riding. In those early morning hours the voice of the liberty-seeking colonists of 1776, the Minutemen of Lexington, seemed to make itself heard in the hearts of Montgomery Negroes, joyously exclaiming, "O, what a glorious morning this is!"

All day long empty buses passed, trailed by white-capped city cops. Very few white passengers rode on that Monday. Of course, 75 to 80 percent of bus riders normally were black. But many of the 20 to 25 percent white riders respected the one-day boycott of black citizens and stayed off the bus, too, to support it. Many whites hauled their maids, cooks, and nurses that day. One bus driver confessed that during a six-hour run he took in only $6.30.

Downtown merchants counted the day's receipts and came up

short, too, especially compared to the preceding Christmas shopping days. Negroes, who as a group had a reputation for spending their earnings without much thought of saving for tomorrow, just "were not in town" to spend money and in any case had no way to carry purchases home. But, then, boycotters were in no mood to go shopping. Christmas was not on their minds. One woman had walked to town to shop for Christmas. She said that while she was in one large department store, the realization came upon her that she was the only black customer in the store, and she hurried out. She stopped in another store and found a similar condition. Deciding that there were no black people in town, she left and went home without purchasing anything.

Only one arrest was reported during the day in connection with the boycott. As one bus approached a bus stop, followed by the "white caps," a small group of curiosity seekers stood near, laughing at the sight. The bus driver stopped at the sign and opened the door, expecting the crowd to get on. Instead, a nineteen-year-old college student, Fred Daniel, full of joy, pranks, and frivolity, took hold of the arm of his friend, Mrs. Percival, and playfully "helped her across the street."

The motorcycle police were upon him in a flash. They accused him of hindering the passenger from getting on the bus and held him until a patrol car came to take him to jail, where he was booked for disorderly conduct. When proof was established that Mrs. Percival was not being hindered from boarding the bus, the young man was released and freed, feeling that "the experience had only helped him to do more for the cause."

That day was rough on the bus drivers. They complained to the police department that they were being "persecuted and molested" in various places by colored children who ridiculed them and stuck out their tongues at them as they passed by.

In response to the complaints, officials asked Negro school principals to "stop the children from gathering on corners and poking out their tongues at the embarrassed motormen." Teachers dutifully instructed the children to go about their business and not bother the bus drivers. The children obeyed, but, when tiny tots saw no one looking, especially their teachers, they stuck out their tongues at the "yellow monsters," then looked angelically ahead of them as if they had not done a thing!

In windows, doorways, and yards, people peered at the huge, empty yellow motor vehicles. The empty buses, each with its pair of white-capped motorcycle policemen trailing behind, evoked count-less memories of bitter past experiences. Suddenly, all the emotions that had been held in for so long were released in heartless taunts, laughter, and hand-waving.

"You wanted your buses, now you got 'em!"

"It's dey buses, let dem keep 'em!"

"Who will you kick now?"

No obscenity was employed. But though the taunts were mild, harmless, they did the persecuted, oppressed people worlds of good.

The *Advertiser* later (January 10, 1956) quoted a report that one seventy-two-year-old man who had ridden the bus for thirty or forty years sat on his front porch and laughed heartily every time a bus drove by. A woman reported gleefully that the buses were driv-ing by her house "as naked as can be."

Yet another woman "who had walked halfway across town" was given a ride by a minister who asked if she was tired. She re-plied, "Well, my body may be a bit tired, but for many years now my soul has been tired. Now my soul is resting. So I don't mind if my body is tired, because my soul is free." All during the first day of the boycott, black drivers during off-hours gave walking boycotters rides. Preachers, lawyers, doctors, businessmen, and ordinary folks picked up people walking; it was said that Ph.D.'s and no d's got to-gether and knew each other as brothers, all members of one race, sticking together for one common cause. A close bond of fellowship and friendship was created. Thus, the race became united. Each person bore his part of the burden. The car owners drove Cadillacs or jalopies, whatever the case was; the bus riders walked if they were not picked up. And the boycotters loved it! They stopped talk-ing so much and so loud on the job and kept many things to them-selves. Petty jealousies disappeared, and they manifested a new trust for leadership. In "sticking with the race," they astounded themselves, as well as the white population, which did not know what had "come over the darkies!"

One white woman fired her maid because the "sullen girl" refused to divulge any information concerning the boycott. Many white women disguised their voices to "sound like voices of black people" and telephoned different ministers to find out where the "pick-up station was," and "if there was any new information that they should know." When the ministers would direct them to a certain church for all the information they would need, the callers would ask "where the churches were and how to get there." Then the ministers would know who the callers were and hang up.

Before Monday was half gone, Negroes had made history. Never before had they united in such a manner. There was open respect and admiration in the eyes of many whites who had looked on before, dubious and amused. Even clerks in dime stores, all white, were more cordial. They were heard to add, after a purchase by a black customer, "Y'all come back to see us," which was a very unusual occurrence. The black customers held their heads higher. They felt reborn, important for the first time. A greater degree of race pride was exhibited. Many were themselves surprised at the response of the masses, and could not explain, if they had wanted to, what had changed them overnight into fearless, courageous, proud people, standing together for human dignity, civil rights, and, yes, self-respect! There was a stick-togetherness that drew them like a magnet. They showed a genuine fondness for one another. They were really free—free inside! They felt it! Acted it! Manifested it in their entire beings! They took great pride in being black.

The Monday Night Meeting at Holt Street Church

Six thousand black people, along with local reporters, packed Holt Street Baptist Church that night, December 5, 1955, for the first mass meeting of the bus boycott. In the main auditorium, the balcony, the basement, the aisles, steps, the front, side, and back yards, and for three blocks up and down Holt Street, people crowded near to hear what was said. Loudspeakers were set up so that crowds who sat in parked cars two blocks away could hear. Police cars patrolling the area warned those inside the church to turn down the volume, which was disturbing the people outside, but no one paid any attention. The volume stayed loud.

White journalists from Montgomery and other nearby places were on hand to report the news of the boycott. Cameras flashed repeatedly, taking pictures of the thousands gathered in the church. So intent were the people on what was being said that the photographers went unnoticed.

The pulpit was jammed with Baptist, Methodist, Congregational, Catholic, and other ministers, and with organization officials. They conducted a spirited devotion of prayer and hymns. Prayers were offered for "endurance, tolerance, faith in God." There were prayers for the city commissioners; for "misguided whites"; for the weak; and for all races and nations. People felt the spirit. Their enthusiasm inundated them, and they overflowed with "powerful emotion."

Reverend Ralph Abernathy, presiding, said the boycott was not a one-man show, nor a preacher's show, but the show of 45,000 black Montgomerians. It was also a show of black Americans all over America and all over the world and of freedom-loving people everywhere. When one ministerial spokesman after another told of the tremendous success of the one-day boycott, cries of joy and thunderous applause pealed forth and "ascended the heavens to God Almighty," as one present was heard to say.

The leaders reiterated that the protest had been and would be kept Christian, non-violent, legal. Even Joe Azbell, city editor of the *Montgomery Advertiser,* seemed impressed, for in his article on Wednesday, December 7, he confessed that "there was discipline among Negroes which whites were not aware of."

When the question was posed as to whether the people would end the one-day bus boycott, thousands of voices shouted the same word, "No! No!" One lone voice cried out in clear tones, "This is just the beginning!" Thunderous applause was the response.

Those on the pòdium agreed, without one dissenting vote, that the protest must continue. Ministers pledged themselves and their congregations to remain off the buses until legal steps were taken that would insure fair, unbiased, equal treatment of all bus passengers. Mr. E. D. Nixon received an ovation when he observed that "Negroes stopped riding the bus because they were arrested, and now they are being arrested for not riding them."

As the *Alabama Journal* reported the next day, the Negroes passed a four-part resolution urging:

1. All citizens of Montgomery "regardless of race, color, or creed" to refrain from riding buses owned and operated by the City Lines Bus Company "until some arrangement has been worked out between said citizens and the bus company."
2. That every person owning or who has access to automobiles will use them in assisting other persons to get to work "without charge."
3. That employers of persons who live a great distance from their work, "as much as possible" provide transportation for them.
4. That the Negro citizens of Montgomery are ready and willing to send a delegation to the bus company to discuss their grievances and to work out a solution for the same.

A committee was appointed to draw up resolutions and to make proposals to be presented to the bus company. For a task of this nature, the regular leaders of the boycott movement tried to distribute leadership opportunities among all the educated members— ministers who wanted to participate, men of Montgomery, even women who were deeply involved and knew what was going on. Thus, a mixed group of this nature, along with a few of the regulars, made up this contingent.

During the afternoon, several clergymen and organization leaders had anticipated this step and were now prepared to present verbal and written resolutions. Since these resolutions expressed the sentiments of the masses present on Monday night, it took only minutes to adopt the measures and to announce that the boycott was continuing indefinitely—until satisfactory replies were received and accepted. One of the ministers summed up the verdict when, at the close of this Monday night meeting, he reiterated that the protest would continue, the car pool would continue, and black Americans, like Enoch, would continue to "walk with God."

The stand which the ministers took on the resolutions proved that they were finally catching up with their congregations. They had definitely decided to assume leadership, so as to give Christian guidance to a rebellious people, and to keep the masses under control. Had the ministers not assumed leadership, disorganized, irresponsible persons might have resorted to shameful violence or individual retaliation upon certain bus drivers. Sparks of potentially undisciplined emotions were in evidence at this first mass meeting, as individuals kept telling and retelling awful experiences they had encountered at the bus drivers' hands. They grew more angry at each telling, and any little provocation could have triggered an uprising. Then a minister would walk up and quietly speak a word of caution.

The Montgomery Improvement Association

Before the meeting adjourned, the masses organized themselves into a new association. It was, without one dissenting vote, given the name "The Montgomery Improvement Association" (MIA). The MIA was pledged to protect, defend, encourage, enlighten, and assist the members of the black community against unfair treatment, prejudice, and unacceptable subordination. To keep down violence, to make the movement Christian-like, and to follow the "passive resistance doctrine" of non-violence, the ministers accepted official positions in the new association as leaders of the boycott. The following slate of officers was elected:

President	Dr. Martin Luther King, Jr.
First Vice President	Reverend L. Roy Bennett
Second Vice President	Dr. Moses W. Jones, M.D.
Financial Secretary	Mrs. Erna Dungee
Recording Secretary	Reverend Uriah J. Fields
Corresponding Secretary	Reverend E.N. French
Treasurer	Mr. E.D. Nixon
Assistant Treasurer	Mr. C.W. Lee
Parliamentarian	Reverend A.W. Wilson

Thus, the permanent MIA was organized and six months later incorporated. All officers were named for one year, but most held their positions throughout the duration of the boycott. After six months, Reverend Bennett left town and was replaced by Reverend Ralph D. Abernathy. Because Reverend Fields could not attend as regularly as he desired, and also because he was at odds with certain aspects of the MIA plans, he was replaced by Reverend W.J. Powell.

For such a tremendous city-wide undertaking, the newly elected MIA officers requested a large executive board of able leaders who could assist in appointing suitable persons to indispensable committees. The MIA Executive Board, consisting of about thirty-five men and women, was appointed by the people. These were persons the MIA members felt would speak out without fear and speak with authority as representatives of the black protesters. They included men such as Mr. E. D. Nixon, known for years to fight discrimination. From the WPC, Mrs. A. W. West, Sr., and I were named.

Although the MIA had regular Monday night meetings at Holt Street Church to sing and pray, it did not always meet for that purpose. Its officers met when important business had to be taken care of. The MIA Executive Board met regularly each week on Wednesday, and if necessary more often. There were often "called" meetings when the board had to cope with emergencies and the next day would have been too late. Nobody complained, tired though we all were. No hour was too early or too late for the members to meet to solve a problem, and no previous commitment except our jobs took precedence over the board's urgent needs. Our time was given freely, for the great cause of justice, and members' personal desires were lost in the total framework of the whole. Nobody thought of what would benefit *him* individually, but of what would contribute to all as a group. There was never a large group of people more dedicated, more consecrated to a cause than these people. Through the tireless, self-sacrificing efforts of the members of the Executive Board, the MIA functioned smoothly.

The drafting of a constitution for the new organization required days and days of thought, discussion, wrangling, and prayerful meditation on the part of the Executive Board, for this framework would influence the lives and welfare of all Montgomery's black citizens.

The leaders of the organization, and the officers who handled the funds, were hardworking, honest, dedicated people who gave their time freely. The MIA had only four paid employees. Mrs. Erna Dungee, who was the financial secretary, worked full-time after the first six months of the boycott. She was a sophisticated, socially involved woman who was married to a professional man and was part of the elite group. She was excellently trained and remained active in community affairs for many years.

Mrs. Maude Ballou was Dr. King's personal secretary; her husband was a college professor. She was a very fair-complexioned young woman, quiet, dedicated to her work and her family. She worked faithfully with Dr. King, and he trusted her completely. She *never remembered* any of Dr. King's business!

Mrs. Martha Johnson was the MIA's secretary-clerk. She worked for all the other leaders of the MIA and took care of their roles in the organization. She never got two persons' business mixed up.

Mrs. Hazel Gregory was the MIA's general overseer. She knew where everything was, never got anything mixed up, and could get what was needed immediately. She had the big responsibility of managing the business, taking care of the building where the MIA was housed, and seeing that it was locked securely at night.

These young ladies worked beautifully together all day, every day, and managed flawlessly. They were also members of the WPC, and assisted the group in many ways. All these ladies were well trained and the most responsible of people. Each one had her own skills and were assets to the MIA. I may add here that these four ladies helped me so much. When I would go to the MIA for any purpose, one of them would stop and help me find what I needed. I loved them all! Hundreds of volunteers assisted, and when they were called to help out, they came immediately.

The MIA rented a very large building, with some five rooms. Dr. King had a private office, as did his secretary, Mrs. Ballou. There was a business room, usually to take care of guests, ministers, visitors, and so on, plus several desks which various ministers could use. Mrs. Dungee had a special room; so did Mrs. Gregory.

Professor James E. Pierce, at the time professor of social sciences at Alabama State College, attributed the amazing success of the MIA and the boycott to good leadership. He stated that the leaders had "finally caught up with the masses." The masses, he said, "have been ready for a long time, but until now they have been without leadership." Among the many people who were essential to the success of the boycott, several individuals played key leadership roles in the boycott movement.

On that first Monday of the boycott, Dr. Martin Luther King, Jr., was elected president of the newly formed MIA. From 1954 to 1960, including the thirteen months of the boycott, he was pastor of Dexter Avenue Baptist Church, where Reverend Vernon Johns had pastored before him. The congregation of Dexter Avenue Baptist had always been made up of many of the elite—the professionals and intellectuals—of Montgomery's black communities. Most of the church's members were well educated, with good jobs and high positions because of their college and university training.

Although he was only twenty-six years old at this time, Dr. King's background had prepared him for leadership. Born in Atlanta, Georgia, on January 15, 1929, his father had succeeded his grandfather as pastor at Ebenezer Baptist Church there. He was academically prepared, having graduated from Morehouse College in 1948 and received the B.D. degree from Crozer Theological Seminary in 1951. He had married Coretta Scott in 1953 and earned his doctor of philosophy degree from Boston University in 1955. He was the only minister in Montgomery with a Ph.D. degree. His brilliance was easily discernable. His vast store of knowledge and his profound intellectuality puzzled many great minds. He was familiar with every great philosophy of the ancient and modern worlds. He knew or was familiar with all the great thinkers of the various civilizations throughout the ages. He seemed to think that it was prophetic that he came to Montgomery. "Destiny decreed it!" When he came to the college to see me I did not see his small stature. I saw the man, his intellect, his profundity of thought and purpose. He could look one straight in the eye and seemingly read that person's character.

He was energetic, persuasive, and willing to take up the responsibilities at hand. He had leadership ability, patience in listening to what others had to say, and the capacity to put people at ease when they talked with him. His kind, humane approach with an audience of one or many inspired confidence.

In many instances Dr. King appeared meek, humble, even boyish among close friends. When he laughed, as he did often, his total personality responded in kind, and his joy was manifest. He loved life. He loved people—all people, and he was comfortable with any audience, educated and otherwise.

I recall one instance when Dr. King was as happy as I have ever seen him, and what caused that happiness is almost unbelievable. A special convention of educators from across the state of Alabama met for several days on the Alabama State College campus. Dr. King was one of the keynote speakers. At the closing of the conference a dinner dance was planned at the only black hotel in the city, and a number of the college faculty, visitors, and community people attended. Although they were invited, Dr. King and his wife went home after the dinner and did not attend the dance.

At the high point of the dance I was called to the telephone, which was anchored on one of the walls of the dance floor. The caller was Dr. King. He wanted to know if many of his church members were present. My answer was in the affirmative. He wanted to know if I would do him the favor of calling a number of his members to the telephone to speak with him as they danced by. My partner and I began rounding them up, and soon a large group of Dexter Avenue Baptist churchgoers were saying hello to Dr. and Mrs. King over the telephone. He was completely happy during that time. I could hear him laughing as he talked, though I did not hold the receiver. It took only little things such as this to make him happy.

I attributed his happiness that night to camaraderie: good will and friendship. I also attributed it to the fact that he felt he had a mission there; that he had been sent for a purpose. He was "old" for his years—in depth of thought, in knowledge, and in rhetoric; he was wise, fearless, "in a hurry." He never wanted to wait for tomorrow, if that same thing could be done today. The mass of knowledge that he had at twenty-six was perplexing—he was a genius in a hurry.

However, he was human, and he could also get angry, especially when human rights were violated. He was to be angry often in the days ahead.

There were other ministers of the boycott whose contributions were just as important as those whose names are often mentioned. These ministers worked in the background, doing the important things that the spokesmen had no time to do. They kept the wheels of the boycott moving. They kept the "Christ" spirit in the angry congregations. They allayed the fears and built up the faith, hopes, and dreams of the people. Many of them drove regularly in the carpool, and offered their churches as pick-up places for boycotting members. Their names are inscribed in the pages of history.

Among the hard-working members of the MIA was Mr. E. D. Nixon. As we have seen, he had been a key leader in the struggle for black people's rights for many years. President of the Progressive Democratic Association, member of the Brotherhood of Sleeping Car Porters, and a former president of the local and state branches of the National Association for the Advancement of Colored People, he was greatly respected by blacks and whites alike in Montgomery.

Mr. Nixon was humanitarian in that he helped so many people, and the community loved him. All the oldtimers felt that Mr. Nixon should be the president of the MIA, because he "could do anything!" Although Montgomery respected Mr. Nixon greatly, as a railroad porter he was employed out of the city and had to be away often.

The MIA presidency demanded trained leadership and full-time work. The president and other officers had to devote much or most of their time to those tasks. Therefore, we felt it would be better if the ministers held the most visible leadership positions. The MIA president, with his committee, had to make decisions to be presented to the masses, whose confidence in him was most important. That person had to be the epitome of self-control, of sympathetic understanding of people's problems and of government policies. That is why Dr. King was considered a well-prepared man. He knew how to deal with angry people, poor people, frightened people, uneducated people. There was no doubt in the people's minds—they wanted Dr. King to lead them.

Mr. Nixon's role in the boycott was a very important one. He missed the fun of assisting the WPC in distributing the notices calling riders off the buses because he was out of the city on his job on Friday, December 2, 1955. However, he alerted his minister, Reverend H. H. Hubbard, to assist the WPC members in any way he could, and Reverend Hubbard did just that.

For the boycott itself, Mr. Nixon, like so many other black citizens of Montgomery, participated in every phase of activity. He worked with every facet of the MIA—with transportation, money-raising, and others. When the boycott ended, he, along with Dr. King, Reverend Abernathy, and all members of the MIA board, decided to ride the bus in a group in December 1956, officially approving and accepting the integrated seating arrangement the courts had decreed.

Irene West had been one of the first women to join the WPC when it was founded. Mrs. West was a wealthy lady, everyone believed, and one of the most prominent women in black Montgomery. She was the wife of Dr. A. W. West, Sr., who was a dentist. That lady spent much of her time fighting for the cause of first-class citizenship. She was a fine woman, a fighter against discrimination, against City Hall, where bigots such as Mr. Clyde Sellers reigned. She belonged to many social and benevolent clubs, and had many friends of the higher echelon. But she had many friends everywhere and on all levels. She loved her children and her family, but she also loved people. She embraced them all. Her goal was to make the world a fair, honest place where all men would be free. She thought of color as only "skin deep," and she felt that neither the white nor the black race would ever be free until all people were free. She worked toward that end for her entire life. And she valued education as the preparation agent that would, with prayer, get a person to the destination of his choice. She *wanted* to help, to contribute in any way she could, because she was humanitarian, and she loved Montgomery. She was blessed by God, and she wanted to give back to people as she had been given to—that is, her prosperity.

Mrs. West was nearly eighty years old when she and I were arrested at the same time and hauled to the police headquarters for incarceration. She lived to see her philosophy materialize, for she maintained good health and worked with the WPC for civil rights to the very end. Before she passed on, she was making inquiry as to the grounds gained for a better world. Despite her eighty years, she was a busy lady and helped every step of the way.

Finances

Continuing the protest necessitated a treasury. A collection taken that very first Monday night at Holt Street Church yielded the sum of $2,000 in a matter of minutes. The spirit of giving was never more generous, and people gave money proudly.

But even at the very beginning, the members of the Montgomery Improvement Association knew that the cost of the boycott would be enormous. Two members decided to do something to swell the contributions presented at each Monday night meeting.

Mrs. Georgia Gilmore, who had once been arrested on a bus herself, became one of the protest's most ardent supporters. She organized a group called "The Club from Nowhere," which undertook to raise funds for presentation each Monday night. Members baked cakes and sold sweet potato pies to workers who had been buying lunch in cafeterias near their work places. Soon workers and even stores waited eagerly for these ladies to bring their foods for sale. The club members approached anybody, and the customers for the delicious sweet potato pies, cakes, and other pastries these women prepared were not just black people, but also white people who enjoyed well-prepared foods.

At each Monday night mass meeting the club leader would present a large cash donation, and the crowd would give the group a standing ovation. The challenge was so exciting and the public attention so rewarding that another group decided to compete with Mrs. Gilmore's organization. Thus, Mrs. Inez Ricks and *her* friends organized "The Friendly Club." It too raised large sums of money, which were also reported at each Monday night meeting.

The two teams, who remained good friends, enjoyed competing to raise the money needed for the movement. They also represented a vital element of each Monday night's entertainment, giving people another way to rid themselves of their frustrations and pent-up emotions. The congregations began to look forward to seeing which group would win each week's competition. Most people, for the fun of it, would contribute to both groups, often giving similar amounts to each in the hope of a tie. But each leader wanted her own group to win, and the two groups put everything they could, including money, energy, and strength, into each Monday night's contest. Each side presented its amount, waited for the reports, and vowed to win the next week.

One thing that had to be established in the minds of all the persons involved—the ministers, the boycotters themselves, and later the lawyers and the courts—was that the MIA was not a corporation of businessmen who profited from proceeds earned! The organization did not make money; there was no business operation on which to make money. It did not offer jobs or buy food for the poor or pay the ministers their salaries. The individual churches did that! Rather, the MIA was an assemblage of people from most of Montgomery's black churches, who came together for the specific purpose of survival! The MIA was *people!*—church people who contributed a part of their weekly earnings for themselves! The contributions were "free will offerings" given by those who wanted to give. Offerings were not compulsory. Nobody kept records of how much each individual contributed, for contributions were taken in mass meetings when thousands put something in the collection of their own free will.

Contributions came from around the world, either directly to the MIA or through various churches whose ministers turned them over to the MIA. At the very beginning, the Finance Committee—a group of volunteers, men of means, honesty, and purpose—took charge of the collections. These "selected persons" received the money, counted it, rolled it up by amounts, and gave it to the treasurer. They accompanied the treasurer to the banking places, where the money was safe in deposits.

Accounts were maintained with the Alabama National Bank in

Montgomery and the Citizens Trust Company in Atlanta. These banks were well known, with references above reproach. The MIA chose to use two banks simultaneously, in order to avoid having too much money in one. There were two different accounts, two different purposes. One bank was a community bank for quick service. It was in a good neighborhood, of reputable image, not crowded, and anxious for honest business. As for the second bank, the MIA was very particular in this choice, for that bank took care of the big money—the thousands of dollars in gifts that came from across the country and the world. The best minds handled this investment, for from this source new station wagons were bought for the walking boycotters. Also, gasoline was bought for the many cars helping to carry workers back and forth; tires and batteries were purchased, and repairs and mechanics were paid for.

The financial secretary and the treasurer of the MIA received the checks, which had to be signed by the MIA officials. Checks written to pay for organization expenses had to be signed by both Dr. King as president and Mr. Nixon as treasurer.

Financial reports were made to the officers and Executive Board on a regular basis. A Finance Committee member checked every receipt of costs and approved the payment after investigating. When all committees' payment results had been checked, and all expenses had been approved by all committees involved, then one of the ministers, most times Dr. King, would report the expenditures to the large audience in attendance at one of the nightly meetings, and that audience would approve the report and approve payment. In fact, one reason *why* the MIA had regular periodic meetings was so that the Finance Committee could deliver its reports. The Finance Committee was authorized to spend money on behalf of the organization, *after* the entire body approved. Also all incoming gift checks were announced and the amounts made known. Thus, every participant knew what the income was, how much was spent, what it was spent for, to whom it went, and how much was left. The darker children were, at last, given the respect that made them feel like human beings.

There was never any doubt whatsoever about the honesty of those leaders in charge. All the ministers were aware of procedural patterns for banking, and at no time during the entire thirteen-month period was there ever a report of theft. Those working with the collections could give account of every penny.

The MIA Newsletter

For a while, at the very beginning of the boycott, the only communication the masses of people enjoyed was what was received from the ministers at church. They had no specific way of knowing what was taking place in their community, and so were "in the dark." Dr. King mentioned a "newsletter" to me one day, and asked if I thought I could spare the time to produce it. All I had to do was put it together, he said; the MIA would reproduce it. I consented. I never knew how to say no! And he trusted my ability. Gosh! How I hate to say that!

I attribute the whole thing to the fact that I was an English teacher. As soon as I had begun teaching my English classes at Alabama State College, the students and I started publishing a monthly college paper that covered the college, the teachers, and the city, reporting interesting news that was worthy of publication. The students took great pride in writing articles that covered the student body, the teachers, and the community, and soon people, including parents, were asking for copies.

In any case, I was attending each Monday night's MIA meeting and serving on the MIA Executive Board, and it was no problem for me to take notes. Then, too, I served on that special "Mayor's Committee" which handled our negotiations with city and bus company officials. I kept notes anyway, according to habit, and enjoyed it. Thus, editing the MIA newspaper was nothing at all. I never got paid. Expenses were reimbursed, but there was no remuneration.

I notified the various sources to keep me informed, so that I could transmit all the happenings in the newsletter. The response was terrific. Often other leaders or members of the board gave me items to include. The news items were "jotted down" on paper, not in organized form. I even had to take some over the telephone. I put that newsletter together as the news reached me. When a month had passed, the newsletter was complete. I did it alone. No big deal!

We began with four legal-sized pages. When I had put my notes into form; arranged the articles for first, second, third, or fourth page; added other facts of the boycott, and gotten the items Dr. King or other leaders of the MIA wished included, I had all the news we needed. As questions increased, we had to enlarge the publication with another sheet of two pages. Before the boycott was finally over, the publication had grown to eight pages. We called it the *MIA Newsletter*.

It took me no more than an hour or two to put the items together, type the sheets, and drop it off at the MIA. Mrs. Dungee and Mrs. Gregory reproduced each issue in mass numbers. The mailing list included thousands of people, for every family whose name was sent to me received the newsletter. Thus, there were as many newsletters as there were families. Also hundreds of copies were mailed out of Montgomery, for they brought in the money from America and abroad.

The plight of the Montgomery people was explained monthly in these pages, and the national and even world-wide response was amazing. In a very short time, money was being mailed to the MIA in large quantities. Any newsletter of pathos brought in thousands of dollars. The news items brought more. Thousands of dollars began to flow into the MIA's treasury and did not cease for thirteen months.

Looking Forward

Our first day had done everybody good, for the angry ones had released pent-up emotions. The maladjusted, frustrated ones "walked off" the feeling during the day's routine and felt better. Those who suffered from inferiority complexes felt important. So there was definitely no stopping it now. The time had come for the black people to stop "waiting on the Lord," and to help God to "make rough ways smooth." The Lord was opening the way; everything had pointed to it. Black Montgomery had to go on! They *wanted* to go on, for the taste of glory was like sweet wine on their lips. For once they were in the driver's seat, and they had made themselves felt. They were "somebody," and they enjoyed the significant awareness of being in a position to dictate policy!

The one day of protest against the white man's traditional policy of white supremacy had created a new person in the Negro. The new spirit, the new feeling did something to blacks individually and collectively, and each liked the feeling. There was no turning back! There was only one way out—*the buses must be changed!*

To continue the boycott, the determining factors would be personal human response; the effect the one-day bus boycott had upon the bus company; and the collective bargaining pressure as a result of the boycott. And as the boycott continued, the weekly Monday night meetings would serve as a communication center for conveying further instructions and for keeping up morale.

But there were groups of zealots who felt a need for meetings more than one night a week. The regular ministerial group felt that one meeting a week was enough and did not go along with the idea of more, but they did not oppose those who wanted more. A second meeting gave those ministers who did not have much chance to preach, the ones who were offering their churches for the purpose, an opportunity to take the leadership. And there were people who could not come to Holt Street Church because of the distance. Thus, a second service a week was conducted on Thursday nights. The MIA approved, for more people got the opportunity to attend two weekly services.

3

Negotiations

Indefinite extension of the one-day bus boycott made negotiations between the bus company and black representatives indispensable. With practically 100 percent of black patrons boycotting now, it was impossible for the buses to continue normal operations. By a little inductive reasoning, the public knew how much money the company was losing daily. In a press statement on Tuesday, December 6, 1955, the day after the one-day protest, J. H. Bagley, the bus company manager, stated that on a rainy day the buses typically had 15 percent less than the normal number of riders. Black Americans normally constituted about 75 percent of the riders, so the boycott meant over five times that 15 percent loss, or five times the rainy day loss of funds. The company was losing possibly three-fourths of its normal intake each day; it could not possibly stay in business.

Despite these facts, neither the bus company nor the City Commission made any effort to meet with Negro representatives to discuss or settle the trouble. And, because they made no move to meet with the blacks, neither did the boycotters make a move to meet with them. The bus company probably felt that it would lose prestige by seeking to negotiate. The three commissioners, following a political strategy that had always led without compromise to a continuation of complete and total segregation, perhaps figured that they would lose votes if they showed anxiety over the situation. The Negroes were too proud to seek them out and also held their peace. Then, too, black people felt that if they were overeager in contacting either the City Commission or the bus company, they would have to take less in any ultimate agreement; their original proposals were already a compromise, and they could not afford to take less than they asked for.

It may seem that my sentiments contradict Dr. King's press statements at the time that "blacks were not seeking integration." Certainly he was not demanding integration. However, the women of the WPC had started the boycott, and we did it for the specific purpose of finally integrating those buses. We were tired of second-class citizenship, tired of insults on buses by drivers who were cruel in order to make themselves appear big. The WPC wanted integration because of the abusive treatment of blacks on buses. Women have always gotten away with the truth. Men lie sometimes to get by. Integration was the ultimate end of our struggle. Can you envision 45,000 boycotters *not* wanting to integrate the buses? We just did not get up on the housetops to yell it and thus make our task a harder one. For the sake of a peaceful fight, we kept silent on integration. We were not obnoxious about it, but quietly demanded it. It was Dr. King who said, "Keep them in the dark."

One last comment: Surely a city officer would deny a black man's request for integration. Segregation was what it was all about. If there had been equality all the time, there would be no need for integration. But there wasn't. That was what it was all about.

Some time passed, and conditions continued as they were. On December 6 the attorney for the bus company, Jack Crenshaw, stated in the press that he was willing to meet with Negroes. But he thought that the group should meet with city and state officials, and not with the bus company. "We are not responsible for the segregation law, but we do have to obey it," he told the *Alabama Journal*. "I have explained that to the boycotters, perhaps six months ago." Crenshaw, however, made no contact with the leaders of the boycott to discuss the bus situation during these first days.

Most of us said after the first meeting with him and Mr. Bagley that Crenshaw was a "little man" in his oratory and in his argumentative ability. His talk was brief, his facts very limited, and any time we asked him questions, he would resort to the *law*. When we informed him of the abusive treatment drivers imposed upon us, he would accuse us of starting the fight. He appeared extremely nervous, in a hurry, with absolutely no feeling for the patrons of city bus lines. I felt very sorry for the man, for he seemed miserable.

The bus company's manager, J. H. Bagley, was a kindly person caught in the throes of a segregated transportation system not of his own making. He was a warm, intelligent person, concerned with his own job but also concerned with the riders who kept those wheels moving. He made a trip to Montgomery's sister city, Mobile, to study the integrated city transit system there. For three days he studied the effect of the "first come, first served" system. Although Mobile was no more than two hundred miles from Montgomery, bus riders accepted that plan with no trouble. In fact, riders never paid attention to where people sat; finding an empty seat and sitting down, or standing if there were no empty seats, was an accepted custom. Black passengers would sit from rear toward front, and white passengers from front toward rear until all seats were taken. That bus system had been in practice in Mobile for a long time, and similar practices were used in Huntsville, Alabama; Macon, Georgia; and other southern cities.

Mr. Bagley returned to Montgomery and reported to the three city commissioners, Gayle, Sellers, and Parks, that the system worked without incident in Mobile and that both whites and blacks accepted the set-up with cooperation and good spirit. But for some reason the local officials did not think such a plan could work in the state capital and refused to try it in any form, even for a trial period. In fact, one official said, "If it were tried for thirty days, or three months, Negroes would not want to go back to the original plan if it became necessary."

Finally, on Wednesday, December 7, the Reverend Robert E. Hughes, the white executive director of the Alabama Council on Human Relations (ACHR), approached the City Commission offering its "good offices" as an organization to arrange for direct negotiations between the aggrieved parties. The ACHR was the state branch of the Southern Regional Council, whose objective was to bring about better race relations. Reverend Hughes; the Reverend Thomas R. Thrasher, a white Montgomery minister and an ACHR member; and Dr. H. C. Trenholm agreed to serve as a contact group. They were able to get the black leaders and city and bus company officials to meet at 10 A.M. in the City Commission chamber on Thursday, December 8.

On Thursday morning the black group met with the two other groups as planned. Mayor Gayle; the two commissioners chosen in the recent election, Frank Parks and Clyde Sellers; bus manager Bagley; Mr. Crenshaw, the bus company lawyer; and news reporters were also present. A special Negro delegation had been selected earlier to serve as spokesmen for the MIA through this period. That delegation was selected by the MIA membership and was composed of Dr. King; Reverends Ralph Abernathy, H. H. Hubbard, A. W. Wilson, and L. Roy Bennett; Rufus Lewis; E. D. Nixon; J. E. Pierce; the two Negro attorneys, Charles Langford and Fred D. Gray; and Mrs. A. W. West, Sr., and me. The three mediators who were responsible for the meeting—Dr. Trenholm, Reverend Hughes, and Reverend Thrasher—were present but took no part in the discussion.

Although our official spokesman was Dr. King, all members of the Negro delegation discussed the various complaints. We announced the three requests in the Monday evening resolutions, which could, if accepted, bring the protest to an immediate end.

The first proposal demanded more courtesy from the drivers. The second request was that Negroes sit from rear toward the front and whites from the front toward the rear until all seats were taken; no one would have to surrender a seat once taken, and no one would have to stand over an empty seat. Our third request was that Negro bus drivers be employed to operate the buses on predominantly black routes.

Dr. King pointed out that the Negro delegation was interested in obtaining not changes in present segregation laws, but greater justice and better treatment for black people on the buses. He spoke of the many tragic incidents over a period of years in which black Montgomerians had been mistreated and insulted by bus drivers. The three proposals, he assured the committee, would work under the segregated patterns.

The city commissioners varied in their responses to the proposals. At first, one of the commissioners stated that they seemed fair to him. But when there was an objection on legal grounds, he quickly underwent a change of mind. The other officials were noncommittal.

Attorney Crenshaw defended the drivers by saying that they *were* courteous, that each driver knew the law and abided by it. Refusing to concede the second proposal, the attorney said it could not be done under existing law. To the third proposal, Mr. Crenshaw replied that blacks did not have the right to tell the company whom to hire, and that the company would hire whom it chose. He said that he did not anticipate the hiring of black drivers in the "foreseeable future."

Mr. Bagley, the bus manager, never opened his mouth except to answer questions that were directed at him. However, questions were seldom directed to the bus manager.

Mayor Gayle and Clyde Sellers were staunch segregationists. Both felt that races should be separated, so that there would be no "sitting together" on buses, or anyplace. For them, complete separation of races on buses, or anywhere for that matter, was necessary. When we questioned "equality" in the separation, Mayor Gayle replied that equality had nothing to do with it.

Mr. Sellers would impolitely interrupt our remarks, show that there could be no integration because the law said so, and attempt to cut us off. Once I persisted and so did he, and for a minute or so, we were both talking at the same time, with nobody in the audience hearing either one of us. He was bitterly opposed to making any kind of concession to improve conditions on city buses for black riders.

Finally, after two hours of talking back and forth and getting nowhere, Mayor Gayle requested that the committee be "reduced to smaller numbers, both white and black." Three additional hours were used up in discussion by this smaller group. But no satisfactory agreement was reached, for neither whites nor blacks agreed to any proposal that was offered. The meeting ended in an impasse. No further meetings were discussed, and things stood exactly as before.

An editorial in the Thursday, December 8, edition of the *Advertiser* gave some wise suggestions to the City Commission. Based on logic and reason, Editor Grover Hall's words drew many letters which agreed with or contradicted it. The editorial read in part, "If Negroes' grievance is confined to that [the request for an altered seating arrangement], then attention should be given to it promptly. Any other grievance should be fairly heard."

If the commission had heeded that suggestion, certainly the gigantic economic loss to the Montgomery City Lines and the city government during the long months of the bus protest would have been avoided. But the City Fathers did not see it that way. Instead, they ignored altogether the suggestions of Hall and many others.

In the first days of the boycott, Police Chief G. J. Ruppenthal told newspaper reporters that his men were investigating a report by the bus company that a .22-calibre slug had been fired into a City Lines bus in the densely populated Washington Park area the night of December 5. Although the finger was pointed at the Negro, blacks doubted the accusation. The ministers had stated repeatedly that the group would refrain from violence, and the congregations were pledged to follow their ministers' lead. There was never the slightest hint that anyone intended to attack the buses or to do physical damage to the company's property. Police investigation revealed no clues to who might have been responsible for the shooting, if anybody, and nobody was ever apprehended. Many blacks concluded that the accusation was only a police hoax.

Shortly after the first attack, a bus driver in the same area said that a large rock had been thrown at the side of his vehicle. There was no damage, and again no one was ever apprehended. Whether the accusations were true or false, nobody ever knew.

Additional reports came from the police department that further violence was being directed against the bus company, but whether there were attacks and whether the attacks were made by blacks, whites, or the police themselves, nobody found out. At one time investigation showed that black areas were the scene of such attacks. Then at other times, white sections were involved. The afternoon *Journal* on Thursday, December 8, reported:

> A bullet narrowly missed a bus driver and his family here last night in the fourth shooting incident reported since Negroes began boycotting city buses. . . .
> Police said a bullet, apparently fired from a second floor, broke

a side window near Driver H. A. Burks. Burks' wife and two small children were the only other occupants of the bus.

Police also said two shots had hit a bus late Tuesday night in a previous unreported incident. The driver said he saw the flashes of six shots being fired from a dark area near a street corner.

The WPC investigated each of the shootings and came up with some interesting data. The shooting referred to above was supposed to have come from a two-story house. The only such house in that immediate locality was occupied by whites. In the last described spree, the shooting came supposedly from a shack on Oak Street, which was occupied by two aged black women who may not even have been aware that black people were boycotting buses. They took no newspapers, owned no radio or television, rode no buses, and were too old to be interested in current events. Since in each of the shooting sprees there had been no injuries and no arrests, many people wondered about the sources of the alleged violence. A .22-calibre rifle was used in each of the shooting incidents. Many boycotters surmised that all the shootings had been done by one and the same person—someone who wanted to make things look bad for the boycotters. But despite the fact that accusations were made, no one was ever held in suspicion or was ever apprehended for the crime. Black boycotters continued to walk in quiet dignity.

At this same time, employees of the Montgomery City Lines agreed upon a two-year pact to avert a pre-Christmas strike. The discussions revealed that in 1955 bus drivers had average salaries between $350 and $360 per month. Under the terms of the new contract, drivers were to receive four cents an hour increase during the first six months of the contract, another increase of three cents an hour for the following eight months, and an additional two cents an hour for the remaining ten months in the life of the contract. This agreement was concluded despite the fact that drivers were driving empty buses.

In the *Montgomery Advertiser* on Thursday, December 8, Manager J. H. Bagley announced that if the bus boycott continued, it would be necessary to "reduce service in the areas where no passengers were riding." Asked how many of the city's seventy-two buses would be put out of service if the boycott continued for any length of time, Mr. Bagley replied, "Well, if business is 75 percent below normal, then—!" He left the sentence unfinished, but his meaning was clear.

On Saturday, December 10, the sixth day of the boycott, the bus company manager announced that some bus service in specific black neighborhoods, where all riders were boycotting, was being discontinued for the time being. Eight bus lines were being cut out; those lines serving predominantly black areas would be halted completely. Now buses would go only into those areas populated by whites, and the downtown section.

Although this news was published on Saturday, actually the service in Negro areas had been curtailed Friday evening, when another .22-calibre shooting at a bus supposedly had occurred.

The cancellation of service was another terrible mistake made by those in authority. With buses on those lines, there was always the possibility that eventually the very tired, weak, indecisive riders, those not particularly in accord with the continued movement, eventually would begin to ride them again despite the same old conditions. For at that time boycotters had not yet gotten into the habit of walking. Sometimes custom is difficult to break, especially in the December cold and rain. But the buses *were* taken off, relieving everybody of the temptation to ride—a temptation that would have been severe when the rains came, and the freezing cold! Now, since no black neighborhoods would have bus service, even if boycotters were tempted to ride there would be nothing to ride on. And with the buses gone, the boycotters snapped themselves into condition for the long, cold rainy periods that followed in that very severe winter season. Naturally, the boycott leaders were very pleased about the bus company's action.

Disappointed over the failure of the first effort to settle the protest, the Alabama Council on Human Relations again attempted to mediate. Reverend Hughes wrote another letter to the *Advertiser,* trying to set the stage for another meeting. It was useless. The boycott continued. Finally, however, Reverend Thrasher, the Alabama council's president, along with the City Commission and the bus company, agreed to meet again on Saturday, December 17, at 9:00 A.M. in the Chamber of Commerce.

At this meeting not only the three commissioners and bus company personnel were present, but also a special committee which Mayor Gayle had appointed to meet with the Negro delegation. In this group were representatives of the Merchants Association, the Parent-Teacher Association, labor unions, the white Ministerial Union, Chamber of Commerce, the White Citizens Council, and the furniture dealers. One of the furniture dealers, a Mr. Tennille, was an outstanding white man of power and influence, who ranked high among the power structure of Montgomery.

Most of the white members of the committee, among whom were unbending segregationists, were pleasant, composed, and gentlemanly. The black committee was also pleasant, capable, and determined. Both sides were well educated and prepared. As I recall such meetings, I remember that there were very few times when one's equilibrium was not under control.

The Negroes who attended the last meeting attended this one as well. A few new members also joined the group, including Mr. Dungee Caffey and Mr. P. M. Blair, who were invited by the three white commissioners. They were selected because they were "yes" men who did "favors" for "special" people and got favors back. These two black men were well-known businessmen. Because they were in business, they probably had to call upon the mayor many times for special favors. And people are human! P. M. Blair, known to whites as Montgomery's "black mayor," was seen as a "yes" man to white people. His business could be closed anytime. Thus, he voted in favor of the whites, and they kept his business open. This was the rumor which Blair never denied. He merely laughed the accusation off. Blair was never invited to serve on Dr. King's committees.

Also present were the legal advisers of the city and the bus company, and K. E. Totten, vice president of the National City Lines, operators of the Montgomery City Lines, who had flown from Chicago to confer on the Negro boycott of city buses.

On the stroke of nine, the Negro delegation entered to discuss its proposals with the largest group ever to meet during the boycott to help settle the protest. For three hours, however, the discussion got nowhere, for the white segment would not accept our three basic proposals. The counsel for the city agreed with the bus company lawyer, Mr. Crenshaw, that the proposals would violate segregation laws. And Mr. Totten agreed with the company attorney, saying that the company was bound to obey city laws. The main black representatives did not vote with Caffey and Blair. Thus there was no vote.

At noon Mayor Gayle decided to reduce the committee to a new low of eight whites and three blacks. The three blacks appointed by Mayor Gayle were Mr. Caffey, Mr. Blair, and only one of the others of the first delegation who had been appointed by the MIA. The remaining three of us appointed by the MIA were left out.

The whites whom the mayor appointed were representatives of the white ministers' organization, the white PTA, the Chamber of Commerce, the labor unions, the merchants, the furniture dealers, and the White Citizens Council. The name of the wcc representative was not given by the mayor at first, but he was added to the list later and became one of the committee members.

The Negro representatives were visibly disappointed and agitated by the mayor's selections, for they felt that this group was racially imbalanced and not representative of the white people of Montgomery. Blacks felt that at least two of the whites would be decidedly unsympathetic toward their cause.

One was the founder of the Montgomery White Citizens Council, an organization dedicated to maintaining segregation by imposing economic pressures on black Americans. His presence made the boycott delegation feel that the mayor had not attempted to select impartial committeemen.

The other objectionable member was a minister who had spoken out publicly against integration in churches following the Supreme Court's decision that school segregation was unconstitutional. The Negro group felt that he would not consider this matter without bias. They felt betrayed by the mayor.

Dr. King, our delegation's spokesman, challenged the imbalance in the number of the two groups and told the mayor that there had to be equal representation if the Negro delegation was to remain at the meeting. The mayor insisted that there were eight whites because there were eight organizations they represented. I replied that there were also eight organizations that were represented by the black group.

Recognizing the finality of the black delegation's decision, the mayor acquiesced. Thus, eight blacks were retained in the group. The eight included Dr. King; Reverends Abernathy, Hubbard, and Wilson; Rufus Lewis; Caffey; Blair; and me. Both white and black legal advisers were present but were not counted as voting members of the appointed committee.

A white minister was elected chairman of the new smaller group and opened the meeting for discussion. Thus, we began all over again, with the same people with whom we started three hours ago.

Beginning the discussion was a member of the white ministers' organization. A most eloquent speaker, he had a commanding voice, which vibrated with profound spiritual emotion. He was tall and muscular. His physique and voice blended perfectly as he stood stately, reverential, almost godly. His very posture commanded respect, and the group sat there beholding him, prayerful that the situation would soon be settled. His tones and words were reassuring, and the black delegation relaxed, feeling for the first time that the causes which precipitated the boycott would be thoroughly studied and remedied.

The speaker spoke of the frailties of man and the infinity of God. It took only a few minutes, however, to discern the direction of his oratory. Before he sat down, he had shown that bus drivers were only human, and, like the riders, were not always up to par in courtesy. The drivers were also discourteous to whites, he said, and both white and black riders might have given drivers cause for discourtesy.

The chairman stated that courtesy was due everybody and that the number one proposal for more courtesy should be accepted and publicized in the local press. The attorney for the company did not see the need for publicizing the "courtesy" clause, but agreed to the first proposal, as did the others present. Thus, the first proposal, that more courtesy be given black riders was unanimously adopted.

The chairman suggested that the second proposal be by-passed for the moment and that the third proposal, concerning hiring of black bus drivers, be considered next. There was protest from the boycotting group, but the third proposal nevertheless was discussed next.

That discussion was useless, for the whites agreed that the company could hire whomever it chose, and that since it was not southern custom to hire black bus drivers, the Negroes had no right to propose it. Thus, that proposal having been disposed of, without a vote, the committee turned its attention to the number two proposal, on seating arrangements. By now it was 12:30; the conference had been in session for three and a half hours. Everyone was tired. One of the white members stated that he could not work under pressure, suggesting that if the black people of Montgomery would agree to end the boycott and go back to the buses until after the Christmas rush, January 15 to be exact, the committee could reconvene and discuss that proposal. He presented this idea as a motion, and the chairman put it to a vote. The eight whites voted for the recommendation. The eight blacks voted against it. The motion was defeated. The chairman adjourned the meeting until the following Monday, when the same group agreed to meet once more and try to reach an agreement.

It was ludicrous to sit there, one highly trained *political* group playing a silly game against another highly trained *intellectual* group, when each side knew what was happening. It was ludicrous, too, to think that the white group was so naive as to think that the black group, all highly trained academically, could not see through their little scheme to get boycotters to go back to the bus.

The black group agreed to return to another meeting only because they wanted to keep options open, not because they felt that a solution would be reached. It was evident that this mayor's group had no intention of trying to reach a fair solution. The meetings were just a front for publicity.

On Monday, December 19, a cold, cloudy day just before the Christmas holidays, the appointed interracial committee met as planned at nine o'clock in the same place, the Chamber of Commerce, to try again to find a solution to the bus protest.

All shook hands, laughed, and chatted together as if they were old friends, and then in a very amiable mood sat down and resumed the discussion. Dr. King asked for adoption of the black riders' three proposals and got a quick second to the motion from the black delegation. The white chairman requested discussion, and that was about as far as the motion got. It was discussed to death.

One of the white ministers made a subsequent motion to reserve seats at the drivers' discretion and to allow each race temporarily to occupy seats in the reserved section until they were needed, but he felt that seats should be reserved. This subsequent motion was seconded by a white person. At this point one of the white ministers had to leave. He stated that he was not able to stay for the discussion on the subsequent motion, but he wanted to cast his vote for it before he left. However, the subsequent motion got lost also in the heated discussion because the Negro delegation charged that the resolution, if voted on, would put the practice right back where it was in the beginning.

By this time it was quite clear that the whites had no intention of making any concession toward a new seating arrangement which was in conflict with the existing segregated pattern, nor did the black leaders have any intention of taking less than full concession to the three proposals presented.

Tempers flared, and the atmosphere trembled heavily with tension. Dr. King stood up and requested the black delegation to withdraw from the meeting. The whites, he said, had come there with their minds already made up to act against the proposals, and further discussion was useless.

Tempers flared again as various members of the committee hotly denied the charge. The chairman accused Dr. King of the same thing. One white woman, who was serving as secretary for the mixed group, stood and in an emotional tone expressed her resentment toward Dr. King for accusing her of having a preconceived notion on the matter. Then she individually agreed to the employment of Negro bus drivers, since "black men were used as white people's chauffeurs." But she felt that 50 percent of bus seats should be reserved for white people, irrespective of how many of either race rode the public vehicles.

His voice calmer, Dr. King sat down, and discussion began all over again. At noon Monday the group had nothing more to show than what was done on Saturday.

The eight whites then agreed to draw up some recommendations which were to be signed by the whites only. These would be sent to the City Commission. These recommendations, submitted to the mayor on January 18 and published in the press, included more courtesy for all riders and reserved seats at the front for whites to be changed in number at the driver's discretion "in proportion to the average patronage of each race." A sign was to be put at the last seat, indicating "white" on one side and "colored" on the other. Such a sign had been removed from transit lines in Montgomery twenty years earlier, yet now the white committee of ministers, PTA workers, merchants, and White Citizens Council members recommended the use of it again.

The recommendations which all eight white delegates signed and sent to the mayor amounted to naught, since the whites had no power to force black bus riders to accept them, or to go back to the buses. Naturally the black delegation did not accept them, and this meeting adjourned indefinitely. The Negro delegation had in any case been instructed by the masses not to meet with the whites again after that Monday, whether another meeting was planned or not.

Since Dr. King was with us at this final meeting with the City Commission, all of us decided that the MIA should come to the front, employ capable lawyers who would take over from there, and permit the courts to handle the matter. That is just what the MIA did. And the boycott continued.

4

The Continuing Boycott

The MIA Transportation System

The Montgomery carpool of 1955 was one of the most effectively planned mass transportation systems in American history. Planned hurriedly by amateurs to fill an immediate need, the system worked with such precision that it became something of an enigma to many observers.

After the first few days of the boycott, taxis no longer worked in conjunction with the movement. At first the cabs had charged each rider a dime, and the MIA had supplemented the difference in the fare. Then local officials had started a "squeeze" on taxis, giving Negro cabs periodic checkups and forcing drivers to collect the regular minimum fee instead of the dime. So for a time there was a total dependence upon private cars. And they worked beautifully.

The bus boycott affected the entire city, and the MIA tried to cover every need. With few exceptions, the rides were free. However, for rides to or from distant areas beyond the normal limits of the city bus lines, a fee was charged. Each day some 325 private cars picked up passengers from 43 dispatch stations and 42 pickup stations. The dispatch stations were designated places where workers congregated in the early morning, beginning at 5 A.M., to be taken to work. From 5 A.M. until 10 A.M., dozens of cars left these points every ten minutes for anywhere within the working radius of Montgomery. The dispatch stations included most of the Negro churches, all of the Negro funeral homes, several clubhouses, stores and other key places where business was being conducted and where people went in and out purchasing things, popular corners, and the eight Negro-operated service stations. By ten o'clock in the morning, most of the workers had been dispatched, so casual hourly pickups were scheduled during the rest of the day. Out of the way places might not be covered except for the early morning carpool.

The forty-two pickup stations became active around 1 P.M., when maids, cooks, nurses, and other domestic workers began getting off. From then until 8 P.M. this service continued. Many of the pickup places were in areas occupied primarily by whites. Thus, grocery stores, churches, school corners, other centrally located corners, and downtown areas were common pickup stations. Among the neighborhoods serviced with free carpool service were Cloverdale, Cloverland, Normandale, Ridgecrest, Oak Park, Capitol Heights, Dalraida, Downtown, Maxwell Field, Gunter Field, and Milbrook Highway.

The two key downtown pickup spots were a Negro-owned parking lot on McDonough Street and Dean's Drugstore on Monroe. The parking lot belonged to a black woman whose family had owned property for years. She "rented" the lot to the carpool, but, I was told, never collected the rent. Dean's was the business place of pharmacist Dr. Richard Harris, an ardent race man. The ancestors of both these owners had been early settlers who laid claim to the valuable sites, clearing and working them, when the city was first established.

These two places were the central exchange points for transfers. All cars worked specific areas and returned to these two stations. If one person was going across town and the remaining "load" was going to town, all of the passengers were taken to Dean's or to the parking lot, where cars going in all directions would pick people up and take them where they were going. A car that brought passengers into downtown would return to its regular run carrying passengers going in that direction.

Dr. Harris kept the cars at his pharmacy moving with all deliberate speed. He created a system that enabled the cars to enter one way, unload, reload, and move away swiftly. Passengers often entered his drugstore and purchased medicines and other supplies, thus increasing his clientele.

Because the sites were private property, authorities did not have authority to molest passengers or to question them there. The two pieces of property were free to the carpool and free to the boycotters. Had it not been for these two black-owned enterprises in the heart of downtown Montgomery, the carpool system could not have given the regular service it did.

The members of the Transportation Committee, led by Alfonso Campbell and Rufus Lewis, did a superb job of mapping out the routes, for Negroes worked in every section of the city, and all got free service. Those who did not get service were too lazy to go to the dispatch stations or pickup places. Or maybe some of them preferred to walk along the streets to be picked up by cars which had not been registered in the carpool.

Very few black drivers ever passed a pedestrian walking along the street without stopping to give them a lift. Our "share-a-ride" slogan received a wonderful response. Even sympathetic whites, both men and women, stopped and picked up pedestrians. Young white drivers would stop and allow walkers to "pile in." One black woman was given a ride to her door by a uniformed policeman. She discovered, however, that he had a motive in offering her a ride, for he questioned her "in a most friendly, jovial, indirect way" about the protest, its leaders, and some of the "secret plans." She was a "dumb one," though, and did not seem to know a single answer to any of the questions he asked. She was most grateful, however, for the ride.

How could 325 car owners give free time and service to a boycott which lasted for so many months? People who worked all day picked up during the early morning hours or late evenings. Those who worked nights picked up during certain hours of the day. From 5 A.M. until 8 A.M. and from 5 P.M. until 9 P.M., many working people could render volunteer service. Few cars were needed during the day, and ample numbers were supplied.

During the first days of the boycott, people used their cars and furnished their own gas free of charge. But as it continued, collections were taken in churches on Sundays and at weekly mass meetings to furnish gasoline. The money was never paid to the drivers, but a certain number of gallons was supplied each driver daily from one of the eight black-owned filling stations, depending on how many hours each driver could devote to the free service. Some received one gallon, some three, some five or more. The integrity of each was trusted, and each was believed to have been earnest and just in his claim and in the service rendered. Of course, some people who drove never availed themselves of this free gasoline, donating it out of their own resources.

Twice a week the Transportation Committee collected the gasoline charge tickets from the service stations and paid for them. Mrs. Maude Ballou, Dr. King's secretary, wrote and banked all checks, after Dr. King and Mrs. Erna Dungee checked them out for accuracy and recorded the amounts. Eventually, after contributions began arriving and money was in the bank, the MIA paid all MIA accounts weekly through its regular checking account, and the service stations encountered no delay in payment. Meanwhile, men of faith kept those stations operating with their own money.

What the boycotters did not know at the time, but would find out soon enough, was that photostatic copies of these MIA payment checks would be made and turned over to the grand jury when it began its investigation of the bus protest in February.

After months of boycotting, individual drivers who had been picking up "walking people" on their way to and from work began to grow weary. To assist the walkers, all of us had driven before, in between, and after working at our own jobs. Exhausted, we were going to sleep at the dinner table with a spoon of food halfway between the plate and the mouth.

Then, like a miracle, money began to flow in to the MIA. When people across the country realized what the Montgomery black people were experiencing as a result of the boycott and the carpool service that was being conducted for them, they sent more money to buy fuel for the motor vehicles. As money poured into the MIA treasury, the Finance Committee got busy paying its debts. The MIA even purchased one station wagon, then another. The MIA began to hire drivers to carry workers to their jobs, or to transfer places where other drivers would drive them to their destination. In addition to money, some people also sent station wagons to be used. Someone in Ohio sent Mr. Nixon a station wagon to use for the boycott; he was to return it later, after the boycott was over. Several of the leading churches were given station wagons to transport their congregations to and from work. These station wagons were new and old, but, even if they were used, they were good ones and were wonderful in carrying larger numbers of riders. The new ones were given freely to be used strictly by churches in giving service to the members by getting them to and from their jobs. The churches could not charge the members for such service, and they were also responsible for the drivers who drove the vehicles. Soon there were six station wagons with drivers paid to operate them. Eventually more than twelve churches either bought station wagons or received them from sympathetic people in various parts of the country.

When this money began coming in and bills had been paid, the boycotters took on great faith. They knew now that they would make it. At this point, when station wagons began to operate in large numbers from five in the morning to ten in the evenings, with paid MIA relief drivers taking periodic shifts, single cars and their volunteer drivers were relieved and did not have to take regular daily runs to give black boycotters lifts. And for the convenience of riders, new routes were mapped out, and a regular schedule was started that accommodated everyone. The system was operated efficiently and on schedule. No more walking to work now! All a person needed to do was to come to one of the many pickup stations, wait a few minutes, and be driven to their destination or a transfer station. It was beautiful! Now Montgomery black people settled down to a long year of boycotting.

A Unique Christmas Observance

During the cold days of December, boycotters walked. The protest, which was to last for one day, had continued. Christmas shopping and heavy packages did not deter blacks from the pledge not to ride the buses again until their demands had been met. Many Christmas

POLICE DEPARTMENT
CITY OF MONTGOMERY

Date   12-1-55   19

Complainant   J.F.Blake   (wm)

Address   27 No. Lewis St.   Phone No.

Offense   Misc.   Reported By   Same as above

Address   Phone No.

Date and Time Offense Committed   12-1-55   6:06 pm

Place of Occurrence   In Front of Empire Theatre   (On Montgomery Street)

Person or Property Attacked

How Attacked

Person Wanted

Value of Property Stolen   Value Recovered

Details of Complaint (list, describe and give value of property stolen)

We received a call upon arrival the bus operator said he had a colored female

sitting in the white section of the bus, and would not move back.

We (Day & Mixon) also saw her.

The bus operator signed a warrant for her. Rosa Parks, (cf) 634 Cleveland Court.

Rosa Parks (cf) was charged with chapter 6 section 11 of the Montgomery City Code.

Warrant #14254

THIS OFFENSE IS DECLARED:
UNFOUNDED   □
CLEARED BY ARREST   □
EXCEPTIONALLY CLEARED   □
INACTIVE (NOT CLEARED)   □

Officers   F. B. Day
           D. W. Mixon

Division   Patrol   Time   7:00 pm
                                     12-1-55

10M - PARAGON PRESS—24551

The police report of December 1, 1955, regarding the incident of Rosa Parks. Courtesy of Black Belt Communications Group.

Motorcycle police watch a black-owned parking lot in Montgomery where people wait for rides. There were almost a hundred of these pick-up stations. Photo by Don Cravens.

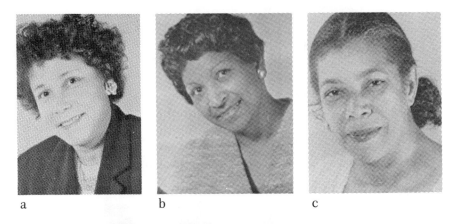

Prominent boycott figures: a) Mrs. Jo Ann Gibson Robinson; b) Mrs. T. M. Glass; c) Mrs. Z. J. Pierce; d) Mrs. Irene West; e) boycott lawyer Fred D. Gray. Photos courtesy of Black Belt Communications Group.

A sample copy of the "News Letter From M.I.A.," issued by the Montgomery Improvement Association, is reproduced on the following three pages. Courtesy of Swarthmore College Peace Collection.

NEWS LETTER FROM

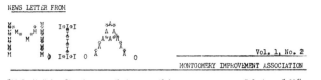

Vol. 1, No. 2

MONTGOMERY IMPROVEMENT ASSOCIATION

530 South Union Street   Montgomery, Alabama   Telephone 5-3364
M. L. King, Jr., President   June 23, 1956

RECENT HAPPENINGS

In the preceding issue of MIA News Letter, mention was made of the fact that a three-judge federal court had outlawed segregation of races on motor vehicles in Montgomery on the grounds that it violates the fourteenth amendment, and is, therefore, unconstitutional. The judges gave attorneys on both sides a period of two weeks to submit suggestions as to how the formal judgment given on the case could be carried out. That means briefly that : 1. The judges could call for an immediate end to segregation on busses. 2. The judges could grant an order restraining the immediate implementation of integration while the defendants__the City Commission, Public Service Commission and the Police Department__appeal the case to the Supreme Court and receive a verdict.

The two weeks period terminated on June 19. The formal judgment halted segregation on busses, but delayed the implementation of integration for an extended period of ten days to allow the defendants time for appeal. Negroes await the final judgment from the two possible decisions with great anticipation. No attempt has been made by Negroes to ride busses until segregation has been completely abolished. The car pool service is still in operation.

Between 30,000 and 40,000 Negroes are being transported daily by the car pool. There are very few complaints, if any, for service is wonderful. Hundreds of people are still driving their cars, wearing out tires and automobiles, re-lining brakes and mending automobile parts. They expend their own energy and devote long hours daily to the cause. They are tired, but they don't complain. They have been faithful for more than six months. They may have to serve many more. Nothing definite will be known for ten more days.

A REGRETTABLE INCIDENT

A month ago the MIA was incorporated into a permanent organization, with some new officers elected to serve the various posts. Prior to this time the MIA operated on a temporary, emergency basis to meet the unprecedented needs arising from the bus protest. Until the recent election, all officers were temporary.

The Reverend Uriah J. Fields, who had served as temporary recording secretary of the Executive Board of the MIA, was replaced by another minister, Reverend W.J. Powell of Old Ship A.M.E. Church. Reverend Fields, a student at Alabama State College, was busy with studies at the college, as well as with his regular pastoral duties at the Bell Street Baptist Church. He could not be present at all meetings and was, therefore, unable to render the type of service that the organization needed. He had not been present for several weeks before his replacement.

Reverend Fields resented the fact that he had been replaced, and in an emotional state, went to the press with false charges against the MIA.

Since its beginning the MIA has encountered much opposition from local authorities and a few disgruntled persons within its own rank. The charges made by Reverend Fields were so preposterous that the Association felt the accusations were unworthy of refutation.

Since that time Reverend Fields has been dismissed by his church, because of the false charges. But, in a spirit of Christ, he has regretted his retaliatory steps against the organization and has apologized to the Executive Board and to the MIA mass meeting public. He has also issued, of his own free will, a statement to the press retracting his accusations.

The Association regrets the unwarranted, false accusations made and also regrets the personal suffering encountered by the minister, who tried to retaliate against, what he later called, "personality clashes" with two men of the transportation committee. Reverend Fields admits with regret, the falsity of his accusations. He is a hard worker and is dedicated to the cause of civil rights. But in a moment of weakness, he lost self control. He was tired, for he has worked with 50,000

2

other Negroes for six months. He was angry and felt rejected. In a state of human passion and human frailty, he spoke falsely against an organization which he loves. The wrong has been righted, but the blur remains. The minister's mistake has been costly to himself and to the good name of the MIA, but 50,000 of his fellow comrades will neither desert nor forsake him. "To err is human," says Pope, "but to forgive is divine."

In the election of permanent officers, Reverend Ralph D. Abernathy was elected to the position of First Vice President, replacing Reverend Roy Bennett, who moved to California. Dr. Moses W. Jones, Second Vice President. Reverend A. N. Wilson, Parliamentarian and Mr. C. W. Lee, Assistant Treasurer. The other temporary officers were elected to regular posts.

ACKNOWLEDGEMENT AND REQUEST

Since the protest started December 5, the headquarters of MIA have had to change location four times before a permanent place could be found. Various methods had to be tested and tried for the emergency before one was finally accepted for keeping records. The situation was entirely experimental. Under the circumstance the organization did the best it could toward keeping records up to date and acknowledge receipt of all mails. Now that a very fine system has been adopted, there will be no delay in replying to the correspondence, inquiries, etc.

The MIA has sent receipts or replies for all monies received, but there is the possibility that some have not received acknowledgements of receipts of funds. The Association, therefore, requests that every individual, organization, or church, that sent money, but failed to receive acknowledgement of that money, to notify the organization immediately. Every penny received can be accounted for by the MIA, for the personnel is made up of the most reliable of people, who are dedicated to the job of securing for Negroes justice. They possess integrity, fidelity and honesty. Negroes of Montgomery are completely satisfied with their handling of public funds. The nation, too, which has been so wonderful in helping to bear the financial burden, should know that all money sent has been used solely for the purpose for which it was sent.

VOTERS' CLINICS

A movement has gotten underway to encourage Negroes to register and to become qualified voters. Hundreds of volunteer workers are contacting non-registered, age-eligible people to exercise their constitutional right to qualify.

There are more than 50,000 Negroes in Montgomery, yet only 2,058 are registered voters. According to statistics, 34,000 Negroes are twenty-one years old and older. Of these, hundreds have tried, but failed to qualify as voters. They feel that voting is a privilege; that it is their constitutional right. Thus, they are going to try again in large numbers to secure their right of suffrage.

DR. MARTIN LUTHER KING, JR. HONORED

In recognition of the outstanding work Dr. Martin Luther King, Jr. has done as spokesman in the great movement in Montgomery, several honors have been given him.

1. The Unitarian Fellowship for Social Justice presented him the "Holmes-Weatherly Award for 1956". It was presented in Boston. The citation identifies him as an "uncompromising champion, and vigorous moral guide to countless people..." in their struggle for freedom.

2. "The Fisk University Alumni Award for Outstanding Contribution in Human Relations" was presented him in Nashville, Tennessee in May. It credits him with uniting "the non-violent, passive resistance of Ghandism with spiritual power of Christianity, which forced an invincible weapon of love to inspire Negroes to walk to freedom and justice, through barriers of intimidations, violence and weather."

Dr. King has justly earned such outstanding awards. He has given himself to this movement, ignoring threats, enduring arrests, intimidations and humiliations of false accusations. He has remained calm, serene, Christ-like. The strain tells on him, however, He looks older than his twenty-seven years.

COMMENTS

Have you received your MIA News Letter yet? Do you have comments you would like to offer? If so please write The Editors, MIA News Letter, at the above address. Suggestions will be appreciated.

REVEREND FIELD'S RETRACTION
(as sent to the press)

June 18, 1956

These statements were issued by the Reverend U. J. Fields who discontinued his connections with the Montgomery Improvement Association (MIA) for the purpose of correcting statements that he had been charged with making concerning certain leaders of the Montgomery Improvement Association.

These statements are being made voluntarily and without being pressured to do so by other persons.

It is with deep regret that the statements I made Monday night, June 11, 1956 about some leaders of the MIA and as to my reason for leaving the organization were misquoted, misinterpreted and misunderstood by people throughout the nation.

Therefore, this is an attempt to set the record straight by re-stating and using my personal signature to substantiate what I have to say about the MIA and its leaders.

First, allow me to state my reason for quitting the organization. I left the MIA because of "personality clashes" with several members of the Executive Board. (Reverend King was not involved personally). Our relations have always been cordial.

Secondly, I said what I did about the "few exploiting the many" and about money being misplaced (not misused) in anger and passion.

Certainly, there is no evidence available to me to indicate that money has been misplaced and there is no proof that money has been misused by the MIA. To my knowledge money sent to the organization has been used only for the purpose of transportation.

Surely, some leaders have enjoyed the privilege of visiting other cities and towns throughout the country, but I have no evidence at all that would allow me to truthfully say that money sent to the organization has not been brought back to the organization.

As for Reverend King, president of the MIA, I hold him in high esteem. In my association with him I have found him to be kind, understanding, honest and a dynamic leader. I feel that his integrity is beyond question, and it is to be regretted that the statements published envolved him as has been observed.

I would like to take this opportunity to offer my apology to leaders of the MIA, Montgomerians, and our many friends and supporters throughout the nation for the statements that have been attributed to me as having said.

It is my desire that you will accept this apology in the spirit in which it has been made. My determination to work for equality, justice and first - class citizenship for all people has not changed in recent months. I shall continue in whatever way I can to do whatever is in my power to hasten the day when democracy will become a living reality for all Americans, irrespective of race, color or previous circumstance.

Signed:

Reverend U. J. Fields
Montgomery, Alabama

Martin Luther King, Jr. addresses a meeting of the Montgomery Improvement Association, of which he was president. Photo by Don Cravens.

Left: A woman balances a box of turnip greens on her head as she slowly makes her way home on foot. People in Montgomery walked dozens of miles a day rather than ride buses. *Above*: Station wagons were bought by the Montgomery Improvement Association for boycotters to ride. The cars were purchased with money sent by people from all over the world. Each wagon was registered in the name of a church. Photos by Don Cravens.

shoppers, not waiting for a pickup, walked and carried heavy, cumbersome bundles in their arms, on their backs, or, as one *Life Magazine* photograph showed, on their heads.

At this phase, the Christmas shopping season, the boycott received very little attention from local news media. The period was nonetheless important to boycotters. In addition to the bus boycott itself, many boycotters decided not to buy from merchants or businesses that Christmas.

First of all, the Montgomery business community had shown little support for the boycott. There had been letters from individuals condemning the inhuman treatment of blacks on bus lines, but not one from any of the corporations who owed so much of their success to black customers. So, individually, many black Montgomerians decided to purchase only essentials such as food and necessary clothing, until the boycott ended. And many decided to trade only with Negro businessmen.

Second, since many boycotters owned no cars and needed buses to reach the big stores in downtown Montgomery, they stayed at home and bought only essentials. Thus, for most of them, toys were out. So were Christmas trees and decorations. There was little or no discarding of faded or tight overcoats, shirts, dresses, or suits. Walking had reduced the sizes of most boycotters, anyway! Also, new furniture some people had planned as a Christmas present to themselves was forgotten. Certainly out of the question was the Christmas replacement of a six-year-old automobile; the old car ran as well as could be expected and was getting them and the boycotters where they wanted to go. If others had promised themselves a renovated home, or the addition of a room, such ideas were cast aside. Following the trend, Negro children learned to make rag dolls and to fix old toys that had been discarded. Passersby could see children playing in their yards with balls that had been taped or wrapped, or with dolls whose heads had been glued on. One child was seen crying on Christmas Day because one of her doll's eyes had dropped down into its head. Her mother promised to fish them out and glue them back on. This seemed to pacify the child, for she stopped crying.

Usually there was eager expectation for festivity at the Yuletide season, but this 1955 Christmas nobody seemed to have the desire to put up Christmas decorations. They did put up those left over from the year before. But, on the whole, people now planned to spend the season more quietly, solemnly, prayerfully. As they vowed to spend less, to learn to save more, and even to sacrifice some things they needed but did not just have to have, black people this year gave no gifts! Friends who were in the habit of exchanging presents asked that the practice be discontinued for this year. Word circulated that all black people should spend the season in meditation and prayer, instead of dancing and entertaining friends.

Thus, black Americans were boycotting the buses intentionally, but boycotting businesses unintentionally. They just were not buying that year. And the more economical they became, the less money the stores took in. According to published reports, one merchant stated that Montgomery's stores took in $2 million less during December 1955 than during previous Christmas seasons.

In addition, white bus riders also had trouble with transportation. The Montgomery bus company had operated buses or trolley cars in the city for more than twenty years, and not for one day had those vehicles failed to run their regular routes. But on Thursday, December 22, under the pretext that drivers were entitled to holidays, the bus company ran the following paid advertisement in the newspaper:

TO ALL RIDERS OF THE MONTGOMERY BUS TRANSPORTATION LINES
Bus service will be halted on Thursday, December 22, 1955, for all bus riders of transportation lines. Such service will be discontinued throughout the Christmas holiday season. There will be no buses operating on any lines in the city or county in the area. Even the bus drivers deserve a holiday period.
(Signed) The Bus Company Manager

Most importantly, when the public transporation service stopped for the Christmas holidays, white bus riders had no way to get to the shopping areas, for whites who rode buses usually had limited funds and no money for taxi service. Of necessity they had to do without some things. Thus, willy-nilly, they were boycotting, too. They did not buy, but it was not intentional!

The merchants began to feel the squeeze. Some businesses began closing or going bankrupt. "Closed" was seen on many storefronts where "Open for Business" had been seen before.

The truth was that the buses had no riders, and the bus company was financially distressed. The company had survived from December 5 until December 22, about seventeen days, almost without passengers. Following the holidays, service resumed on routes in basically white areas, but the continuing loss of revenue was tremendous.

According to Mr. Bagley, eight lines were completely discontinued. Thirty-nine bus drivers were laid off or dismissed when service was first cut. Dozens of the huge transit vehicles sat lined up in the car lot at the northern end of McDonough Street. There was no need for them. One day passersby saw the giant buses being used to help a private company pack down some newly built-up ground. The few buses still in operation underwent route cuts and changes and ran much less frequently than the previous seven-and-a-half-minute intervals.

According to the black bus company workers, there had never been more than four Negroes working in all. According to one of them, they held the general "flunky" jobs such as "handy" men. However, when the wholesale layoffs began, the black men were among the first to go, for whites who had tenure took over their menial jobs. Regular drivers chose to become flunkies or handymen rather than go without work altogether.

When these black workers were dismissed, the kindly Mr. Bagley interceded with other firms to get three of them placed in other jobs. He spoke well of them and expressed regret that they had to be laid off.

One December day a very aged black woman, who was struggling along on foot, walking with a cane, was overtaken by a bus with a lone black rider on it. The bus stopped at the stop sign just ahead of the old woman, to let the black passenger out. Seeing the situation, the crippled woman hobbled along faster toward the bus. The driver, thinking that the woman was hurrying to get on, seized the opportunity to show how courteous he could be to black people if they would only ride again. So he called out, in a very friendly tone, "Don't hurt yourself, auntie, I'll wait for you!"

With anger and scorn, the old woman pantingly, gaspingly called up to him as she hurried past the open bus door, "I'm not your auntie, and I don't want to get on your bus. I'm trying to catch that nigger who just got off!" Then she drew back her cane to strike the rider as he fled beyond her reach.

So at Christmas, when there should have been peace and good will on earth, there was in Montgomery each race's suspicion of the other. There was no open demonstration of this suspicion, but one could see it in the sharp glances that followed persons as they passed each other on the streets, in stores, or at the laundry. In crowded elevators, where Negro and white rubbed shoulders, or in lines at the post office or bank, the chill was there. The suspicion!

Since the bus company management had given the bus drivers and their empty buses a holiday, buses no longer rattled by as people walked along in the biting cold and rain, carrying heavy bundles of food and practical needs in their arms. Everybody knew that it would be a long time before black people again rode the buses. But nobody anticipated at the start that another full year would pass before the situation was resolved.

In mid-December 1955, the black people of Montgomery were calm, proud, content, and strangely peaceful. They faced the birthday of Christ with grim determination to continue their passive resistance.

And then came Christmas Day!

On this holiday, December 25, 1955, a long paid advertisement from the MIA appeared in the local papers. The ad explained the purpose of the organization, the position it had taken in connection with the boycott, the fairness of the black citizens' request for improved seating conditions. It spoke of the human dignity of all mankind, and of the need for a better understanding among all peoples, especially among the races. Its tone was conciliatory, but the article assured readers that black people of Montgomery would never, of their own free will, return to the buses without positive improvements. The ad ended with a prayer for peace on earth and good will to all mankind.

Headlines blazed the Negro protest across the pages of large newspapers around the world. There seemed hardly a spot on the globe where civilization extends that did not carry the news. According to hundreds of reports from reporters who represented large newspapers and magazines across the world and who visited Montgomery, oppressed people the world over took heart and became more optimistic that their own fate could be improved.

Black Montgomerians took heart, too. They no longer complained of exhaustion after long walks. As the City Fathers remained obstinate in their resolve not to yield to the blacks' requests, many of the boycotters vowed never to ride the bus again, integrated or not!

5

White Reactions
to the Boycott

As the bus protest continued, with no indication of any immediate solution or compromise, it became the talk of the town. White people who had been indifferent before were becoming interested, aroused, vexed. White reactions to the boycott varied widely. Despite white officials' calls for white solidarity in fighting it, many whites saw the justice of the Negroes' demands for better treatment on the transportation lines and wholeheartedly supported the boycott.

Mrs. Frances P. McLeod, a very kind, understanding white person who was affiliated with a number of humanitarian civic organizations, wrote a letter to the *Advertiser* in December 1955 in an attempt to create better public opinion, which she hoped would help to solve the problem:

> The situation in our city regarding the treatment of Negroes on our city buses has caused us to bow our heads in shame.
> Why could not our city provide such laws for all citizens as do some other Southern cities—Nashville, Richmond, and we understand Mobile? These cities have a first come, first served law. Thus all citizens have equal opportunities for a ride. We hope this problem will soon be solved and that the welfare of all citizens will be a responsibility for all of us.

Another letter to the editor, which appeared in the *Advertiser* on December 9, came from Mrs. I.B. Rutledge, a leading white civic worker who was well-known in religious, civic, cultural, and educational circles. Her letter centered on the spirit of humanitarianism, which asserts that all people are human; all feel hunger and pain; all are made of flesh and blood, mind and body; all have hearts; all suffer when mistreated. Mrs. Rutledge wrote:

> Several years ago I was the only white person occupying one of ten vacant seats at the front of the bus. Standing back of them the car was packed with Negroes returning from the day's work. "Why," I asked the driver, "can't you let these people sit down?"
>
> "I don't mind," he said, "but I'm afraid someone will criticize me."
>
> In the years since this incident, in which I have talked about the bus situation, I have yet to find one white person who feels that it is right that a Negro be made to stand that a white person may sit.
>
> We in the South like to think of ourselves as a courageous people with the courage not only to face danger in war, but the moral courage to face issues and adverse public opinion. Isn't it time that those of us who really believe in Christian and democratic principles of consideration of others and of fair play speak out and help create a public opinion which will make possible a solution of the present situation that will be satisfactory to all? The bus company must move within the framework of the law, but much improvement can be made if the public demands it.

Another white person who wrote the *Advertiser*'s editor, with tragic results, was Miss Juliette Morgan, a librarian at the Montgomery Public Library. Well-informed on local, national, and international events, Miss Morgan was also a keen student of literature, highly intellectual, even brilliant, yet humanly understanding where ethnic groups were involved. I had been at several human relations meetings with her and found her to have a beautiful personality, profound reason and thought, high intellectuality, and concern for humanity. She was somewhere between thirty and thirty-five, I would say, and spoke without an accent. She had met many black people whom she recognized as intelligent human beings, and she treated them as such.

Miss Morgan's letter to the editor, published in December 1955, revealed her respect for black people as decent human beings, just as members of other races are. "It is hard to imagine a soul so dead, a heart so hard, a vision so blinded and provincial as not to be moved with admiration at the quiet dignity, discipline, and dedication with which the Negroes have conducted their boycott," she wrote. "Their cause and their conduct have filled me with great sympathy, pride, humility, and envy. I envy their unity, their good humor, their fortitude, and their willingness to suffer for great Christian and democratic principles, or just plain decent treatment." Her style was elegant, her thought profound.

Immediately after the publication of this letter, Miss Morgan began to get an unending stream of terrible telephone calls, frightening noises at her door and windows, and, wherever she went, hisses, boos, slurs, threats. Angry white people threatened her night and day, promising harmful retaliation. She was threatened with loss of her job, her friends, her few possessions.

For a while she ignored the threats, thinking they would go away. But instead, they increased. The telephone rang almost incessantly. Then her doorbell began to ring, more and more frequently as the sun surrendered its light to darkness. Pebbles were hurled against her window panes far into the night, awakening and frightening her, or preventing her from even getting to sleep.

The telephone calls, threats, and loss of personal friends were too much for the beautiful but frail young lady. One morning, a year or so later, she failed to answer the telephone, and close friends began to worry. When some of them went to see about her, they found her dead. She had taken her own life.

This lovely lady had faithful friends of all creeds and colors, and their grief was immense. Her loss was such a terrible waste— to Montgomery, to Alabama, and to the world. Her death touched the hearts of all Montgomery, and many still remember and mourn her death.

Another newspaper item also resulted in great suffering for its subject, the Reverend Robert S. Graetz, a white minister of a black congregation in Montgomery. Tom Johnson, a reporter for the *Advertiser,* interviewed Reverend Graetz, taking notes concerning his ministry, his family, and his background. He was pastor of Trinity Lutheran Church, active in the boycott, and he aided his congregation in getting to their jobs by helping to transport them in his car.

Johnson also learned from the minister, who was a member of the MIA Transportation Committee, the mechanics of the bus boycott. Then, on January 10, 1956, he published all this in the newspaper.

Immediately Reverend Graetz began getting threatening telephone calls at every hour of the night and day from white people, even children. His family's suffering was almost beyond human endurance. Because he pastored a black church, angry white people would try to frighten him in various ways. Prowlers visited the Graetz home, breaking windows and making verbal threats which could be heard a block away. The intruders went to the bathroom in front of his front door and left human excrement on his steps. No matter how many times he changed his telephone number, callers found out and threatened him hourly, day and night. He, his wife (who was eight months pregnant at the time the newspaper article appeared), and his two young children saw no peace.

The Clifford Durrs, too, were to become martyrs to the boycott. A white lawyer and his family who worked without prejudice with black leaders during the long boycott, they were publicly scorned and socially ostracized.

On the other hand, many letters to the *Advertiser's* "Tell It To Old Grandma" column suggested how strongly many whites opposed the boycott. On December 15, Mrs. K. A. wrote:

> In my travels to other cities in the United States I have always boasted of the amicable relation between white and colored races in Montgomery. I feel that these same conditions would have continued to exist, if those Northern agitators of the NAACP had not sent speakers down here to influence the colored population against the whites. I am heartily in favor of segregation, being a "born and bred Southerner." But the Montgomery Negroes who wish to vote, claiming they are good citizens (when they advise defiance of segregation laws), are urging rebellion against the laws of Alabama and Montgomery. Whether the Negroes consider the law unjust and unfair, it is still the law of Montgomery and Alabama until repealed. . . .
>
> The preachers tell the deluded people, "you are sinning against God; you are sinning against the future of your children, if you do not obey the mandates of the NAACP." As long as we have to live in the same city and depend one upon the other, at least we could have pleasant and amicable relations.

And Hal Lindsay from Georgiana, Alabama, contended that:

> The white people of Montgomery are typical of the other white
> people of America, slow to anger and slow to make up their minds.
> But once they do they have always come out victorious. . . .
> Where is your appreciation, your sense of duty? Look around
> your home. Who furnished the "know how" to build your homes
> and furnish them? Who furnished the "know how" to prepare your
> foods and medicines, give you electricity, make your clothes, design
> and build your cars and every other convenience you so richly enjoy,
> that goes with civilization. Now what have you done for yourself?
> You are indebted to the white people of Montgomery for life
> itself, as the white doctor brought most of you into the world. The
> white man paid about 95 per cent of your education, furnished you
> jobs and a place to live, etc. Now suppose the white people of
> Montgomery would not hire you any longer or give you a place to
> live where would you go or do [sic]?

Because the city's daily newspapers were important shapers of
opinion in the community, blacks looked anxiously to their editors
for fair treatment. But it only took one editorial in the *Alabama Journal* to keep us from expecting help from that direction. Published
on December 18, the editorial read:

> Either fortuitously or with a purpose, Montgomery, the first
> Capital of the Confederacy, has been made a guinea pig for the great
> sociological experiment.
> The contributors to this experiment have been the Supreme
> Court of the United States, the NAACP, the ADA and a bunch of wild,
> well-financed political radicals jealous of the South's peaceful and
> serene way of life. . . .
> We have been placed in the national spotlight by a boycott of
> the transportation system, though normally our courts frown upon
> boycotts as violations of law.
> We have been in the national eye as the scene of professed
> and hypocritical Gandhi-ism.
> We have been the scene of national forums with busybodies
> from other states encouraging disruption and ill-feeling among
> our people.
> We have seen money poured into Montgomery, thousands
> upon thousands of dollars, to encourage strife and resistance to nor-
> mal life in our community. . . .
> If envious enemies insist upon using us as a guinea pig for
> alien psychological and sociological experimentation let's not be too

impatient, though we know beforehand the experiment is going to be a dismal failure.

We hoped for better from the *Montgomery Advertiser,* however. Its editor, Grover C. Hall, Jr., was widely read, an erudite scholar with an unusual vocabulary. He sometimes played on words with such pedantry that those with curious minds were sent scurrying to the dictionary. And Mr. Hall was a humanly disposed person; there were times during the strife when he showed a great heart, a kindly nature, and a generous spirit.

According to reports, his father, Grover C. Hall, Sr., had been of the same fine spirit, except that the elder Hall's attitude remained constant. There was, and perhaps still is, a large plaque in an upstairs office of the *Advertiser-Journal* commemorating his humanitarianism toward the minority group.

Sparks of the father were often exemplified in the son. Yet as the boycott struggle continued for weeks, then months, this side of Hall, Jr., was seldom seen. There were times when he lashed out unmercifully at the darker race on his editorial page with taunts, ridicule, play-ups of crime and juvenile delinquency, and pro-segregation precepts. For such, many black citizens wrote angry letters accusing him of yellow journalism and of not being fair in his editorials. He did not seem to mind the letters; he was quite friendly and respectful when members of the boycotting group called upon him. Throughout the boycott, he was both for and against; he praised and he criticized.

I had one occasion to visit Hall, Jr., when I was a faculty member at Alabama State College. The institution was expecting a group of educators, who would be on the campus for a few days. Since journalism was one of the areas of discussion, three of us were invited to make an appointment with Mr. Hall to inveigle him to speak to the group. He was handsome and most courteous, friendly, and helpful; he gave us materials to hand out on the subject, but he did not find it possible to be present. He was a busy man; maybe that was it.

The city editor of the *Advertiser* was Joe Azbell. A reporter of facts as he saw them, he did not try to destroy character or make anyone a saint. He reported the truth as he saw it. Thus, his articles enjoyed a large reading audience. The public respected him for his straightforwardness, honesty, and sincerity. Not only that! His reporting "helped" those he wrote about, and people respected him for his writings and his manner of presentation. This does not mean that he shunned the truth, for he revealed the facts. However, he did not "play up" the worst at the expense of the fact.

The reasons for the whites' mixed reactions were complex and reflected the complexities of the southern social structure. To begin with, whites continued to depend upon blacks to prepare their meals, see after their children, and take care of their homes. Negro domestic labor was cheap, for many blacks were unskilled domestic workers. And even if these workers were skilled, they seldom if ever were paid standard wages. Some black maids got as little as two dollars a day, with hours extending from eight to five o'clock. The average amount seemed to be fifteen dollars a week. Some very good cooks got twenty, and truly excellent cooks boasted salaries of twenty-five or thirty dollars weekly. One said she received as much as thirty-five for her delectable pastries and such. Besides, she "even took care of some business for the madam" and really "ran the house and kids, too."

Because of the color of her skin and the texture of her hair, almost any white woman at that time could get a job for fifty dollars or more a week, no matter how limited her education was. Jobs for clerks in dimestores, cashiers in markets, telephone operators were numerous, but were not open to black women. A fifty-dollar-a-week worker could employ a black domestic to clean her home, cook the food, wash and iron clothes, and nurse the baby for as little as twenty dollars per week. And, with all housework, baby care, and laundry taken care of, there would still be thirty dollars clear. One can easily see why white teachers, who made three to four hundred dollars a month, could very well afford to haul a maid or pay an extra dollar for transportation.

The black domestic workers were loyal to those who employed them, and were dependable and trustworthy in the white homes. It was a common occurrence to hear a young black woman talk about "her white lady." Also, many of the maids and cooks had been with such families for years and actually "felt a part of them." They were loyal to their employers and loved them. White wives were grateful for the services their house workers rendered. The "good" white employers increased the so-called twenty cents bus fare to taxi fare. Some also increased wages. A number of domestic workers informed me that their employers often put extra money in the pay envelopes to put in the MIA collections at the Monday night meetings.

One such maid stated that she loved her white employers as she did her own family and felt that they loved her, too. The wife would often "slip a few extra dollars" in her hand for the boycott movement without telling her husband. At the same time the husband would leave a few extra dollars for the boycott under her purse in the kitchen where she kept it while she worked. Then, when neighbors visited this home to deplore the boycott activities of the audacious blacks, the man and wife joined in the conversation as if they felt the same way. When she, the maid, was called in to bring food or drinks to the guests, each of the two hosts would wink at her to assure her that they were merely being polite hosts.

Similar reports came to the WPC from other workers in private family or public employment whose employers were sympathetic toward the cause and contributed to its maintenance and promotion.

The attempt to break down the machinery of segregation and white supremacy was frustrating. It actually required tearing out the roots of the white man's ideologies, his very life, leaving him insecure, afraid, panicky, desperate. This fear was the force that made him so bitterly opposed to integration of buses and, in fact, integration of anything.

Perhaps this explains the great urge to organize the White Citizens Council, whose purpose was to preserve segregation. And how was preservation to come about? Some suggested such concepts as "nullification" and "interposition." In answer to a question posed by southerners in Washington, President Eisenhower said that he had taken an oath to uphold the constitution of the U.S.; nullification or interposition would not be acceptable under the constitution. James E. Folsom, governor of Alabama, called the terms "hogwash." He recommended to the people of Alabama, and therefore to many WCC members, that the only way to preserve segregation, if it could be done at all, was through a constitutional convention. Then he said that if he were authorized to secede from the Union, because he was governor he would have to do it.

How the wcc planned to keep the races separate in all branches of the total social structure, including schools, parks, and so on, would remain to be seen. The wcc had flourished in Mississippi after Emmett Till's murder, and they were beginning to spread in Alabama.

Selma was one of the first cities in the state to organize such a group, and it started with appreciable numbers. There a Negro grocer, Mr. John Smitherman, had been boycotted out of business by white producers after a misunderstanding between a few whites and Negroes there. Mr. Smitherman was not able to purchase anything in Selma anymore, except one brand of soda pop and milk from one dairy. According to the grocer, all other companies refused to sell him produce. He was forced to close shop, and without another form of livelihood, he moved away. It seems that whites believed that boycotting by one race was right, just, and legal, while boycotting by another race was illegal and punishable by law!

When the bus boycott began, the White Citizens Council was a very small organization in Montgomery. It was just getting started and had few members. Those few members were on the alert, however. They had already seen that the blacks were the ones who had been keeping the buses in Montgomery operating, that more than 75 percent of the riders had been black, and that many whites, too, were boycotting to sympathize with black boycotters' protest. And the wcc did not approve of the situation. On Thursday, December 22, ironically just before the great celebration of the birth of Christ, the local wcc decided to move. It expressed its disapproval in a paid political advertisement meant to divide the boycotters: "Wake Up and Ride the Bus." The newspaper ad implied that the boycott was over. This announcement, of course, fooled no one. Then, on December 30, the group announced that it was offering a $100 reward for the apprehension of parties guilty of violence to city buses.

According to the press, when the wcc was first organized in Montgomery, three hundred nondescript members joined. Among those who constituted the roster of the wcc were the "failures," the "illiterates," the "never-do-well," "non-achievers," "those disappointed in life." None of the important people—merchants, doctors, lawyers, or outstanding men of recognition—had affiliated. But there were also the wcc "leaders," highly intelligent, who believed they could become the highest echelon of the organization, and in so doing become the leaders of the "in" group of the white social fabric. The press also revealed wcc plans to inveigle responsible leaders of the white community into joining their organization, to "put black people, once and for all, where they belonged."

It is useless to deny that black Americans were afraid! Many of them went home early at night, shut their doors, turned out the lights, and tried to sleep. Men got their guns and placed them conveniently near their beds. Some of the women came up with the idea to cover all windows with dark blankets so that lights inside the house would not show outside. Many plans were devised by which people could live until this era passed.

Well, I got my weapon, too. And the cartridges! I was afraid to shoot the pistol, but it was a comfort to have it there. I could not "load" the weapon, because I was afraid I would shoot myself, but somebody loaded it for me. If anybody had attempted to break in, I am sure I would have used the gun.

And then one morning, as I dressed for school, my neighbor rang the bell, handed me a note, and hurried away to her job. I finished my chore, turned out the lights in my home, and was about to leave, when I suddenly remembered that I had not read the note. I stopped, picked it up, and read it:

JOIN THE WHITE CITIZENS COUNCIL
White Only
Before it is too late.
Help to preserve segregation in Alabama.

Repeated solicitations appeared in the daily press, using notices like that one. The wcc members did not have long to wait before this strategy began to bear fruit.

6

The Get-Tough Policy

The New Year Begins

In January hell itself seemed to break loose in Alabama, shattering the very foundations of segregation.

In Tuscaloosa, Negroes were about to invade the University of Alabama campus for the first time. The courts had authorized Miss Authurine Lucy and Mrs. Polly Ann Hudson, two young Negro women from Birmingham, to be admitted to the university for the second semester, and they and their attorney, Arthur Shores, were on the campus conferring with the dean of admissions about enrollment procedures.

Almost simultaneously, the Interstate Commerce Commission handed down a decision that segregation in interstate travel was unconstitutional and ordered the removal of discriminatory "Colored" and "White" signs.

And in Montgomery the boycott was in full force. It had crippled service; created unemployment problems among the many laid-off bus drivers, four Negro company workers, and other personnel; and put tremendous economic pressure on downtown merchants.

Sellers Joins the White Citizens Council

As the boycott continued, the White Citizens Council membership swelled. At one WCC meeting in January, one of the three City

Fathers, Commissioner Clyde Sellers, the police commissioner, made a dramatic entrance into the organization. As Mr. Sellers entered the door of the large city auditorium where the meeting was being held, the platform speaker was discussing the fact that many whites did not team up with the wcc because they had Negro customers.

"Well, *I* have no Negro customers," the police commissioner announced loudly, as he walked before television cameras down the long aisle to the platform, supposedly to join the group.

Naturally there was great rejoicing in the wcc. Mr. Sellers was one of the very first municipal officers or men of distinction to join the fold in Montgomery. If Mr. Sellers was looking for fame, he was not disappointed, for he became the most talked about man in the county. Newspaper and television reporters broadcast the tale widely.

The boycotters read about the action, saw it on television, and discussed it in meetings. Many prayers must have been prayed the night following that announcement, for everybody felt that the police commissioner's action constituted an open threat, and nobody could possibly anticipate what future action might be leveled at the boycotters. But Mr. Sellers' act, which was meant to terrorize black people, only drove them closer together, made them more determined than ever to stick together and to follow leadership, to the very end.

A week later Negro leaders decided to try once more for a settlement with the City Commission. Dr. King arranged an appointment with Mayor Gayle. When people asked Dr. King why he chose another conference with the mayor, knowing his attitude, he stated, "We have to keep trying." But after two hours of discussion, neither side had given an inch. The meeting ended, and the boycott continued.

At these times, after almost two months had passed and with no end in sight, groups of widely-read pedestrians, picked up along the way and carried home, would get into deep conversations when their faith wavered in the balance. Indeed, one must wonder about the peculiar turns that things take sometimes, and about the controlling force that may compel them. Call it fate, destiny, a trick of nature, or the will of God, there is an inexplicable something, a force or power that seems to direct men's lives and twist them into some particular shape. Sometimes that shape is good, sometimes not so good.

During such periods of intense suffering—and people did suffer, mentally, spiritually, and financially—there were those weary souls who began to question God's presence, to wonder where God was and if God was really with the whites on segregation. Even the white man's religion, some said, seemed to be based to a great extent on segregation and white supremacy. Then some mused, "Is God white?"

So they would reason as we drove along, going home from a hard day's work. "Whites were born into, and have lived a lifetime enjoying the role of the superior, feasting their egos on the belief in racial supremacy. To these people, blacks are not equal."

"Yes, those folks don't believe in racial equality, and because of that belief, they think that black people can exist on less than the whites can."

"Separate but equal is right, but it's this separate but unequal that is killing us."

"In the separate schools, libraries, recreational parks, types of employment, salaries, waiting rooms, drinking fountains—no matter what—there has not been equality."

Many of these people had become disillusioned with life itself and wondered at the hypocrisy of it all. How could one set of human beings be so cruel and inhuman to another set, just because of the color of their skin and the texture of their hair? Was it because the side in control *was* superior? Or were whites afraid that, if the other side was given a chance, *it* would prove superior? Was the white man really afraid of the black man?

Most of the drivers who picked up pedestrians as they walked along, tired and hungry, would find a way to bring them out of such moods. We would tell a joke on "whitey" that showed him in a less exalted position than someone had just pictured him in, and everybody would laugh. In no time they would have forgotten the ugly mood they were in and begin all over again.

"God hears our prayers, and in his own good time, he will deliver us. *So don't give up.* For when the time comes, God will make the rough ways smooth! We are going to win this thing. Just you wait and see! So, child, don't give up now. Hang in there!" Before they reached their destination, they were laughing as if that mood of faith had been with them all day.

And hang in there they did. Black citizens were psychologically attuned to the time. Most of the time they were bold, calm, and fearless as never before. The few who were not attuned to the movement were frightened into cooperation by the whitecapped policemen on the first day of the boycott and by a guilty conscience or shame thereafter. But everything, including Commissioner Sellers' entrance into the WCC, seemed to fall in line, to fit in place, as if some force had guided or directed it.

The first seven weeks, four in December, three in January, had been the glorious beginning weeks of the boycott. Walking people had been thrilled over defeating "whitey" and were not tired yet. But then they realized that the situation might go on indefinitely, and it was no longer *fun*. What if this situation did go on forever? The beginnings of tiredness made them reassess their plight.

Some of the boycotters had put in as many as sixteen hours daily, working on jobs, driving in the carpool, and trying to take care of their homes. Some—a small number, three or four, a dozen— were so tired that they were actually thinking of compromising and going back to the buses, feeling that the protest had at least taught white Montgomery a lesson and convinced them that black Americans would tolerate no further abusive treatment. A few of these weak ones even considered a tentative time for an official announcement, and some of the drivers began to hint at it to their riders. These weak ones were some of the followers, certainly not the movement's leaders who had gotten the thrill of boycotting. They were among the poor, with limited means to live upon, and their "official announcement" meant telling their comrades that they were tired of walking and wanted the boycott to end.

Among those who urged an end to the boycott were those who were totally, personally involved among the "walking contingent."

They were the few who depended entirely on the movement, and who were so very tired. The reader who has no personal knowledge of the long distances common laborers had to walk to get to their jobs, unless they got rides, may feel that these people were traitors! Not so! Remember that until the boycott transportation system got established, many people did not get picked up. In the beginning, many "walking people" had long distances to go before they were picked up and given a lift. (Once the MIA transportation system got underway, however, it was even better than the city transportation lines, for the "pickup" places were nearer their homes.) But at first, they walked. If they got a ride, all the better. They were not traitors! Just sufferers! Just plain, ordinary people. That is all.

Then it happened! Commissioner Sellers joined the WCC. As radio, television, and telephone blared the news, it was even suggested that, since Mr. Sellers was the police commissioner, the police force would be an arm of the WCC. All black boycotters rallied at this announcement. Talk of compromise abruptly ceased. Those who were tiring suddenly found renewed energy. Those who had complained of aching feet and painful backs were revitalized. Instead of becoming alarmed and fearful, the boycotters resented the fact that a public official, who had taken an oath to a public trust, would forsake ethics and defy the duties of his office. His joining the WCC had no intimidating effect on blacks. Their reaction was the antithesis of fear; rather, they were inspired to hold out, to stick closer together, to continue to endure whatever suffering was in store. I put my car in the garage and walked. It gave me a sense of sadistic pleasure. I suffered with my colleagues and peers. Their determination was phenomenal, unbelievable. Some vowed never to ride another city bus, whether our terms were met or not!

Some force seemed to be behind this bus boycott in Montgomery. Even in the beginning, the time was right for the protest. Strange as it may seem, this was the year when the bus company had to renew its franchise. The old one, taken over in 1936, expired on March 8, 1956. Yet when the protest began, nobody had had the least idea that this was the case.

On January 18, the city approved a ten-year bus franchise to replace the old one. There was a major difference in this new franchise, though. The old one granted twenty years before had contained a forfeiture clause allowing the city to acquire all rolling stock and properties without payment, if the company closed operation. No such clause appeared in the new franchise. Since company spokesmen admitted that the company was losing money each day of the bus protest, many people wondered if the city would lose its bus service altogether. But neither side gave in, and, despite the public officials' pronouncements, the bus protest continued.

Announcement of the Get-Tough Policy

That same day, January 18, Police Commissioner Sellers announced a "get-tough" policy to force boycotters back to the buses. He made a statement at the Montgomery Junior Chamber of Commerce to the effect that 85 to 90 percent of black bus riders would go back to the buses again except for the fear they held of the leaders. It was, he added, "the boycott leaders who would attack boycotters, or anybody who advocated going back to the bus again without some satisfactory changes in the system." However, no blacks believed him.

On Wednesday, January 25, Sellers announced that he was instructing the Montgomery police department to "break up congregations of Negroes who had been loitering in white residential districts." These "loiterers," of course, were maids, cooks, and nurses waiting at pickup stations for rides. "A person has a perfect right," Sellers said, "to wait for a ride, but the practice of six or eight Negroes huddling together for periods of time, trampling on lawns, and making loud noises in white residential neighborhoods must cease!" He even accused those domestics of becoming "hitchhikers" as they walked along streets and accepted rides. He stated that the police department did not "intend to allow the hitchhikers to become nuisances in white sections."

Commissioner Parks made a public statement that the commission could not allow Negroes to "destroy the transportation system of Montgomery," and reported that a number of businessmen had promised him that they were "going to lay off Negro employees who were being used as NAACP instruments in this boycott."

The Phony Settlement of the Boycott

On Saturday evening, January 21, 1956, a group of federated women—thirty-three members of the Agnes J. Lewis Club—was meeting at the home of Professor and Mrs. J. E. Pierce. Dr. Archie Lacey, then science professor at Alabama State College, had just finished speaking on "The Role of Women in a Changing Society." Then the telephone rang.

Talk stopped, as if everyone there just *felt* that trouble was brewing. All eyes followed the hostess as she answered the phone. Everybody sat forward as she called me to the receiver. Breathing seemed suspended while the members listened.

Dr. King was on the line. Mr. Carl T. Rowan, staff writer of the *Minneapolis Tribune,* had telephoned him from Minnesota to ask for verification of an Associated Press release stating that the bus protest in Montgomery had ended. The wire service had reported that a group of three ministers had met that day with the Montgomery City Commission and had agreed to go back to the buses under the same conditions that had driven us from them.

Dr. King, who was of course the elected spokesman for the boycotting people, now told me on the phone that he personally knew nothing about any meeting with the City Commission, nor who the ministers were who had met secretly with the commissioners. None of us at the Pierces' did, either. Dr. King had confessed his ignorance to Mr. Rowan, and also his surprise that such news should have reached Minneapolis without Negroes in Montgomery being aware of it. We suggested that Dr. King call the *Advertiser.* He did and was told that the story had been released from the City Commissioner's office and that the terms of settlement were being carried on the *Advertiser's* front page the next day (Sunday).

In the meantime, Mr. Rowan called city officials and was informed that the report was true, that three Negro ministers—Baptist, Presbyterian, and Holiness—had negotiated. The journalist was kind enough to call to Montgomery again to assure Dr. King that the boycott had ended.

Confused and greatly disturbed, Dr. King was calling the Women's Political Council together, as he had called the ministers and other key laymen together, to see if anybody knew anything about any meeting with city officials. No one did. Then everybody got busy. Every participating preacher and club president in town was contacted, and within a few hours the entire black population had been alerted. Soon Associated Press wires were correcting the error, and the situation was under control even before it got out of hand.

The three ministers had been identified: Reverend Kinds, pastor of the South Jackson Baptist Church; Reverend Moseley, assisting minister of the Presbyterian Church; and Bishop Rice of the Holiness faith. These three had no active part in the boycott movement. Although the national announcement listed them as "prominent ministers," the truth was that they were leaders of very small congregations.

When these gentlemen were contacted, they told Dr. King that they had been "hoodwinked" into attending the meeting. They had been contacted by someone on behalf of city officials to come to a meeting at the Chamber of Commerce to discuss *insurance.* But when they got there, the discussion centered around the boycott. The men themselves publicly admitted to the Associated Press that they had attended the meeting by special request and that they had refused to take part in the discussion of the boycott because they were not the chosen representatives of the Negro masses. They said that they were totally ignorant of what was happening and did not know that they were supposedly there to "end the boycott." Their refutation of their part in the Saturday meeting was broadcast all over the country.

The City Fathers tried to save face, however. After the refutation by the three Negro ministers, the officials made a public announcement stating that "there must be two factions of black boycott leaders." Then everybody knew why such tactics had been resorted to. It was a feeble attempt to split the solidarity of Negroes.

Boycotters had been tiring again, and many perhaps were thinking of yielding to pressure and going back to the buses. But the news of this incident stimulated everybody. It bound the black population by stronger ties of solidarity. There was no faction now, no division. Never was the boycotting group more unified, more determined to stand firm in defense of justice!

Thus, the article that appeared in the *Advertiser* on Sunday, January 22, 1956, caused nobody to ride buses through ignorance, thinking that a settlement had been reached. Black citizens were happy to walk to church that Sunday morning.

The Mayor Ends Biracial Discussions

The public announcement that the three black ministers had admitted being "hoodwinked" into attending the meeting called by the City Fathers seemed to infuriate the commissioners, for they felt that they had been exposed to ridicule by their own efforts. The first thing the other city commissioners did was to follow in the footsteps of Police Commissioner Clyde Sellers and openly join the White Citizens Council.

On Monday, January 23, Mayor Gayle stated publicly that he was "fed up with biracial meetings" and announced that there would be "no more discussions between the whites and the Negroes until the latter were ready to end the boycott." He added, "We have pussyfooted around with this boycott long enough."

On the one hand, the mayor stated that "white people do not care whether Negroes ever ride the buses again." And on the other hand, in an effort to make them ride, he publicly urged white Montgomerians to halt the practice of using their cars as taxis for Negro maids and cooks who work for them. He told whites that Negroes were "laughing at them behind their backs" for permitting them to serve as "their house help and chauffeurs." He requested the white employers to "cease paying Negro maids, cooks, nurses 'blackmail money' in extra weekly transportation fares in any shape, form, or fashion." He said that such money (which amounted to one dollar per person per week) was extorted under the threat of "not showing up for work" and was used to "pay taxi fares" so workers could stay off the bus. "Any aid the whites give to help to carry Negroes, even for one block, helps the boycott," he warned.

The mayor did not get much cooperation from this angle, though he got some. A few women stopped hauling their maids; some few stopped giving the extra dollar car fare each week. A few housewives not only withheld the extra dollar, but fired those who did not ride the bus. In one instance a maid was fired by one woman for "not riding the bus," and as she left the house she was hired by the next-door neighbor.

But in comparison with the number of maids who continued to draw the same salaries and the extra dollar, very few whites responded to the mayor's call. One maid was fired because she *rode* the bus at the start of the boycott. Her employer told her that "if she could not be loyal to her own people, she most surely would not be loyal to her employers!"

The mayor's proclamation halting further discussion on the boycott brought forth a letter to the *Advertiser* from Dr. L. H. Foster, president of Tuskegee Institute. The letter from the college official was long, scholarly, and was directed through the newspaper's editor to municipal officials and the city of Montgomery. Dr. Foster listed examples in history where injustices had been imposed upon people, showing that *right* had always won in the end. He asked the officials to take note of changes taking place in America and the world. He pointed out the changes that had already taken place within Alabama and the states bordering it.

Boycotters felt that such a letter from one official to another would surely open white people's eyes to new thought in determining fair decisions for all concerned. However, the letter, which brought such pleasure to so many readers of the *Advertiser,* did not affect decisions at all.

According to City Editor Joe Azbell, "a tremendous ovation was heaped upon the City Commission for its stand in working toward ending the boycott talks." City Hall Switchboard Operator

Katherine Brown and Mayor Gayle's secretary, Mrs. Kate Barnett, confirmed a recordbreaking number of telephone calls, telegrams, visitors, and messages, all commending the commission's stand. If there were any calls, letters, or telegrams against the stand, the commission never acknowledged that fact publicly.

Commenting on the response, Mayor Gayle said, "The people are with the Commission. They have proved it today. We are going to hold to our stand. We are not going to be a part of any program that will get Negroes to ride buses again at the destruction of our heritage and way of life."

Commissioner Sellers added, "I am convinced beyond any doubt that every right-thinking white man and woman in Montgomery is solidly behind us in our stand."

Mr. L. R. Grimes, chairman of the Montgomery County Board of Revenue, endorsed the City Commission's policy and said, "We must make certain that Negroes are not allowed to force their demands on us and pull such tricks as this boycott without the whites standing up for their heritage and way of life."

And Commissioner Parks, too, felt that "our people want leadership in this matter, and we, the City Commission, have resolved that we will furnish that leadership."

According to Editor Azbell, many white Montgomerians made the statement that "our governor, Honorable James E. Folsom, ought to take a stand like that, instead of siding with blacks."

White Citizens Council Grows

Reactions to the commission's stand on the bus situation made themselves felt in different ways. For example, white Montgomerians rushed to respond to the call of the White Citizens Council. State Senator Sam Engelhardt of Macon County, who was president of the wcc, welcomed large crowds of prominent members into the fold. The very same day the mayor halted boycott discussions, hundreds of people joined the wcc. A picture in the *Advertiser* showed busy volunteer wcc workers recording memberships and fees. As numbers increased, blacks prayed.

Attorney Luther Ingalls, a wcc spokesman, told the *Adver-tiser's* Azbell that Negroes would never again be able to use the threat of a "bloc vote" on a candidate running for office in Montgom-ery County. Council members, he said, could "outvote Negroes five or more to one. And," he added, "we are only starting."

Mr. Ingalls meant what he said. Two months later, on March 27, the wcc held a mammoth public meeting at the city auditorium, where records were created on 104 candidates up for election or re-election in the May primary. Two thousand people were present to hear the candidates' views on segregation and to take notes on those candidates who, according to the spokesman, "failed to give the right answers." If one of the candidates was not present, his or her questionnaire was there to speak instead. If the candidate was not there, and the questionnaire was not there either, *that* spoke, too; failure to reply was taken as an admission, an answer.

The candidates present were asked the following questions:

1. Are you for segregation?
2. Are you for the mixing of the races in the public schools?
3. Do you want the Negro vote?
4. Do you favor denying the Negro his right to vote?

There was never a question on candidates' character, competence, or citizenship. The wcc's requirements for election were simple: the candidate had to be a segregationist and willing to deprive black people of their rights of citizenship.

Only fifty-one candidates answered the questionnaires or came to the meeting. But evidently all those answered in the "right way." The television report was a thing to see. One man in particular made a statement that probably gained him many wcc votes. He said that he did "not want a nigger vote, nor a colored vote, nor a Negro vote."

Perhaps he had seen the voters' list which had been prepared for publication in the very next afternoon's *Journal*. There were eleven pages of qualified white voters, numbering an estimated 25,000 for Montgomery County. There was one page of black voters, numbering 2,026 in all. This meeting showed that the wcc meant to break the back of the already scant black vote. With 25,000 whites and 2,000 blacks, one can easily campaign on a platform of white supremacy and racial hatred.

Police Harassment of Boycotters

Things really got hot in late January, as the police began to enforce their commissioner's "get-tough" policy. Hundreds of black motorists were stopped, searched, questioned, and given tickets for traffic violations. People who had never been accosted by policemen before were declared guilty of speeding or failing to recognize red lights, caution lights, or stop signs. Some were even accused of failing to ease up on a yield sign, staying too long at a stop sign, or not staying long enough. I myself received seventeen traffic tickets for all kinds of trumped-up charges.

The number of passengers riding in a car became an issue, and some were arrested for carrying too many people on the front seat. Drivers were stopped, searched, questioned, and in many cases given tickets. Fines ran from two dollars up. Many paid up to $22.00 for "speeding." According to television reports, within two weeks' time sixty-four black drivers had been arrested and put in jail for minor traffic violations.

In this latter group was Dr. King himself, who was arrested and put in jail, allegedly for driving thirty miles an hour in a twenty-five mile zone. The minister, accompanied by a friend, Professor Robert Williams of Alabama State College, had been by the downtown parking lot to get a load of passengers and was driving away from the lot toward South Jackson Street. They were stopped by policemen who habitually stood at the entrance of the parking lot to nab drivers as they came out with their loads of passengers. Dr. King and Professor Williams were questioned, and when they showed their drivers' licenses, they heard the policemen whisper among themselves, "This is that King fellow." The police allowed the minister and his passengers to drive away, followed them to South Jackson, and stopped them when the car paused to put out the riders. The police informed Dr. King that he was under arrest for going thirty miles an hour in a twenty-five mile zone.

As Dr. King got into the officers' car, he asked Professor Williams to notify his wife. Then Professor Williams drove Dr. King's car away, as the police took the minister to jail.

Dr. King was held in a cell for only a short time. Reverend Abernathy went in to bail him out and was told that he had to get a statement from the tax office first. "But it's night," he protested, "and the office is closed."

"Well, wait until tomorrow when it opens," was the reply.

But within minutes, hundreds of boycotters were milling around the jail. They did not look too pleased either, for their spokesman was locked up inside. People kept coming, coming, coming! In a very few minutes, Dr. King was released on his own signature, without paying a dime. He was told to come to trial on Saturday. He went and was found guilty and fined. He appealed the case, but later he paid the fine.

Many of the laid-off bus drivers were deputized as extra policemen. This was not announced publicly, but former bus riders, who had come into daily contact with the bus drivers, recognized them immediately and informed the MIA. These idle drivers patrolled the areas where pickup and dispatch stations were located, harassing and intimidating black drivers, questioning them, taking the license tag numbers, examining their drivers' licenses, taking the names of passengers, and trying to ascertain whether they had insurance. Sometimes one car was held up for thirty minutes. In information later given to the grand jury, Mr. Richard Jordan stated that he was stopped and questioned twenty-six times.

Quite often city officers sat in a car across the street from the parking lot, looking on. Many of the Negroes recognized them, and one snapped pictures, just for the record.

Many sad ramifications of the get-tough policy occurred there at the parking lot. For example, one public school teacher was stopped at the lot by a policeman. When questioned by the officers, the teacher replied that he was an American citizen, that he had constitutional rights. For such effrontery he was slapped in the face, his arms were twisted, and he was put in jail. His companion, another teacher, told the ministers about the man's ordeal. However, when the first man was released from jail, after paying a fine, he never told anyone of the encounter. Although he tried to act normal, he was never the same after that. At the end of the school year, he withdrew from the school system. He never explained why, but those who knew of his experience with the police felt that the man had to get away from all reminders of his bitter experience with the law. He moved away from the city, and nobody heard from him after that.

One black taxicab driver failed to display certain legal papers on his cab's window. The driver was ordered to drive the cab and his five passengers to the back yard of the jail. The driver was taken inside and locked up. The arresting officer returned to the cab for the keys. His eyes glared contempt. As he took the keys and turned to re-enter the house of punishment, one of the passengers asked, "Officer, must we wait here for the driver?" He muttered as he walked away, "He's in jail. You can sit there all night for all I care."

The Hate Campaign

Whether it was intended or not, the commissioners' stand against the boycott had started a hate campaign. Only when the three City Fathers joined the wcc and started the get-tough policy did tension begin to rise and attitudes start to change. Whites began staring at Negroes as they passed by in crowded cars. Some would harass blacks who walked along the streets. "Walk, nigger, walk," whites commonly called as they rode past.

Young white teenagers contributed their share to the hate campaign. Cars filled with white youngsters would drive through black neighborhoods and squirt water from rubber balloons upon Negro pedestrians. After a week of water squirting, the water was changed to urine; as it sprayed faces, hair, suits, or dresses, black children and adults had to return home to clean themselves of the stench.

Some speeding cars threw rotten eggs, potatoes, and apples, as well as other objects that not only messed up the victims' appearance but brought physical hurt as well. A teenaged black boy was walking along the sidewalk one day when a carload of white male youths drove past. One threw out a looped rope in cowboy fashion as at a rodeo and tried to catch the boy's head in the noose. Luckily the boy saw it and ducked in time. The loop glanced off his shoulder without injury as the car, filled with laughing youngsters, sped away.

Someone in another speeding car hurled a brick into the back of a Negro boy as he walked along. It hurt him badly, but he was not able to get the car's license number.

Then there was the Negro amateur boxer who walked home from one of the mass meetings. He was beaten unconscious by a carload of young white men who stopped him as he walked along. He was hospitalized for a time.

One interesting observation during this time was the display of Confederate flags. Many of the white youngsters who rode through black neighborhoods had Confederate flag stickers on their cars. People about town displayed the tiny flags on cars, suitcases, and so on. wcc members displayed them on their coat lapels at the city auditorium meeting, which was televised. For a long time as he broadcast the news, an analyst at a local television station kept a Confederate flag on his desk.

One cannot truthfully say that white youngsters were the only ones reflecting the "hate" mood and retaliating in some foolish way. In an article on juvenile racial unrest, City Editor Azbell reported that a white girl had been knocked down, her dress torn, and her books scattered by a group of black children. Moreover, a group of young blacks had thrown bricks at white youths as their cars stopped for a signal light.

Rumor had it that young Negro pranksters looked through telephone directories and copied down many of the names of white women, then telephoned them and frightened them with foolish threats. It was easy to do, because all the names of white women were listed with titles of "Miss" or "Mrs." and could be readily identified. It was the local phone company's policy not to give titles with the names of black women. Even this discriminatory practice had repercussions.

The telephone became a prime channel for threats for everybody. The leading black ministers who had active parts in the protest were not able to sleep nights for the ringing threats of white people. The ringing nuisance began with Reverend Graetz. As we have seen, this white Lutheran pastor of a Negro congregation was also one of the carpool drivers. Whites pestered him, his wife, and his children so much that he had to have his telephone number changed.

The torturing gave Dr. King and his wife, Coretta, no peace of mind; even their young daughter showed nervousness from the incessant telephone ringing. Reverend Abernathy and his wife secured the help of neighbors in answering the telephone. Fred Gray, one of the main MIA attorneys, was pestered and threatened. All the MIA Executive Board members had telephones ringing far into the night, with angry voices delivering nerve-shattering and frightening threats. Many black people left their telephone receivers off the hooks at night so they could sleep. And Commissioner Sellers stated through the press that many Negroes threatened him by telephone to such an extent that he had to put a police guard in front of his house nights for some degree of comfort.

Several crosses were burned around town, but blacks ran to the scene much too rapidly for comfort; after a few efforts when some of the guilty ones were almost caught, this type of intimidation stopped.

Quite a few whites showed effects of the tension. One day I hurried into a supermarket to make some purchases. Not looking where I was going, I accidentally bumped into a white woman shopper. A spasm of hate spread over the woman's face as she drew herself up to soaring heights, as if she had grown a foot taller. She glared at me in contempt. But I reached out and touched the white woman's arm, and in a pleading tone said, "Oh, please forgive me. It was my fault for being in a hurry and not looking where I was going. *I am so sorry!*"

Slowly the hard, cold expression in the steel-blue eyes softened. A slow smile touched her thin lips. "Of course," she replied. "No harm's done." With understanding smiles, we two women, one white, one black, went our separate ways, having narrowly averted what could have been an ugly scene.

Reverend Bonner once drove up to a red traffic light and stopped beside a car driven by a white woman. Suddenly she began cursing him, calling him obscene and profane names, some of which he had never heard spoken before. Reverend Bonner did not part his lips to her, but he said later that he had looked at her quietly with great pity and breathed a silent prayer that "God might give her peace of mind."

Black Efforts to Improve Their Situation

In late January, the MIA Executive Board appointed a committee to file an application with the City Commission for a franchise to operate jitneys for black riders, which would transport them over the main city routes. Such an application was filed on Friday, January 27, by Rufus A. Lewis, J. E. Pierce, J. W. Bonner, Thomas Gray, and Ronald R. Young.

The application was turned down by the City Commission, without a hearing. Mayor Gayle spoke for the three commissioners when he received the application: "If the Negroes want to ride a public vehicle, they can ride the city buses. There is an abundance of public transportation in Montgomery for those who want to use it. If there is a group of people who don't want to use this public transportation, that's their fault. We stand firm in our position that the white people of Montgomery are not going to be coerced by threats and demands from Negroes now or any other time!"

The commission drove a hard bargain. It would not react reasonably to an acceptable seating proposal; it would not grant blacks a franchise to operate their own buses; and its get-tough policy was hitting where it hurt most. Hundreds of dollars were being paid out of black people's pockets for trumped-up traffic tickets and fines.

Perhaps it was because blacks had suffered so terribly on buses that they refused to be moved by threats of arrest, trumped-up charges of traffic violations, and other intimidations. But although they were further than ever from going back to the buses, they were very tired, and something had to be done. Car owners were tired of paying traffic tickets which they knew were helping the city replace the income lost by the decline in bus patronage.

Things were really bad by this time. According to the media, thousands of whites were joining the White Citizens Council. Commissioner Seller's get-tough policy was at its height, and Negroes felt that they had little or no protection from the police force. The MIA sent telegrams to the state's attorney general, John Patterson; the governor of Alabama, James E. Folsom; and other key people nationally, asking for some kind of protection. Mr. Patterson was leaving the city that day, he said, but he promised to look into the matter upon his return.

Some months later, four of us—Dr. King, two other ministers, and I—succeeded in making an appointment to talk with Governor Folsom in person. As we drove to the Governor's Mansion, we wrote down some of the problems we hoped to discuss with him. We wanted his guidance in handling the problems, which were being forced upon us and over which we had no control.

When we were ushered into the governor's office, Governor Folsom was waiting in a room so huge that it seemed to swallow us. He stood to receive us, shook hands, and invited us to sit. Four chairs had been placed around his chair, and we all sat down together. Dr. King started the conversation by telling the governor about our current situation. The governor listened quietly, intently; took some notes; asked a number of questions.

He even teased me, a woman, for being involved. I informed him that I was president of the Women's Political Council and that our women were involved; of necessity, I had had to become involved. I explained to him that both men and women were suffering during the boycott, and that the get-tough policy of Police Commissioner Sellers was hurting black drivers.

Dr. King explained a number of things that were really hurting black Americans in Montgomery. The two other ministers spoke and answered a number of questions that the governor asked. Finally, Governor Folsom spoke. He seemed "filled up" for the moment, sad. Pondering. "The boycott is still in operation," he said, "and does not help the cause any. It has proven its point. Maybe if you decide to go back to the bus, all the other problems may be dissolved. For as long as the boycott is in operation, the police will continue to annoy and pester you." He seemed to think for a moment, then spoke again, "You have proven your point," he said, and he looked at each one of us slowly, seemingly to convince us that stopping the boycott was the thing to do. We thanked him, and left.

As we left, I had the feeling that the governor of Alabama had as many problems as we had. We saw that he was powerless to do anything about the boycott, and we had to stand firm and continue it, even if we had to appeal to the national government of the United States of America. The three men, ministers of God, outstanding in leadership, shining lights in their own spheres of worship, had already decided, even before they were asked to commit themselves, to continue the boycott. If they quit now and stopped the boycott, they would never have the opportunity again! For now, the people were ready! Each of them said so.

In sum, the governor had received us kindly and given us sound advice; tension, which did not help our cause any, was high; the boycott had proven its point; perhaps the best solution was for black citizens to agree to go back to the bus.

This point had been raised and seriously considered by the MIA Executive Board, which was fair in considering every point presented by some of the boycotters, but as always the decision had to be made by the masses, who had to ride those buses. And when all the ministers, club presidents, leaders of various organizations, and the masses in general were approached with the subject, they answered emphatically, "No!" They answered negatively to every proposal that meant going back to the buses without total integration. They vowed that they would never, never, never go back to the buses under the present segregation laws.

Dr. King's House Bombed

On Monday night, January 30, 1956, a bomb was thrown on the porch of Dr. King's home while he was away attending a meeting at the First Baptist Church. The explosion shattered the front glass window, split a porch section, and made a hole in the porch floor. Dr. King's wife, Coretta, and their two-month-old daughter, Yolanda Denise, were in the house, along with a church member, Mrs. Roscoe

Williams, who stayed with them while Dr. King was away. None of them was injured, save for shock.

A white man had been seen getting out of a light-colored automobile, running part-way up the walk to the King's home, which was located about thirty feet from the street, and throwing something against the screen door. He then jumped back into that car and sped away. The lone witness, Mr. Ernest Walters, says it happened so quickly that he had no time to get the license number.

As soon as the Kings' home was bombed, someone called me. Others were being called. We were told to call still others—to get the message out. I called a few, but was too upset to continue. So I went to the Kings' house, arriving about ten minutes after the call came.

In a few minutes an estimated 300 to 500 people, black and white, had jammed the South Jackson Street block where the Kings lived. Cars came from everywhere. Mayor Gayle and Commissioner Sellers rushed to the scene.

Police arrived in a jiffy and in force, and took command of the situation. They tried in vain to move the crowd from the bombed area. The crowd was dangerously quiet, and the air was tense. One of the policemen called out, "Please go home, folks, nobody is hurt." Not a soul moved; no one spoke. The silence was accusing, maddening, threatening, and police officers showed their fear of the hundreds of black people who stared at every move they made, every step they took. These people were silent; they just stood there staring at the police, the city commissioners, the bombed porch of the civil rights leader. Once or twice an officer cleared his throat to speak, then changed his mind and said nothing.

Finally one of the officers again asked the crowd to disperse, and from the angry mob came an answer, "We will, when you tell us which one of you did it!" The policemen tried to ignore the remark and continued to plead with the masses to leave and go home. But everyone ignored them. Nobody moved.

In about fifteen minutes, Dr. King came running up, shocked, out of breath, and apprehensive. After investigating the condition of his wife and child, he came out on his damaged porch, where the air still smelled of dynamite. He waved to the crowd for attention. The crowd stood still. Then, surrounded by Police Chief G. J. Ruppenthal, Fire Chief R. L. Lampley, Commissioner Sellers, and Mayor Gayle, Dr. King began to speak in a calm voice. A respectful hush settled over the audience. The police stopped their futile efforts to disperse the people and listened to the minister's persuasive tones.

"It is regrettable that this has happened, but we must remain peaceful, for we believe in law and order. Don't get panicky; don't get your weapons. He who lives by the sword will perish by the sword. We are not advocating violence. Love your enemies." As Dr. King spoke, a gentle, relaxing stir was heard and felt among the crowd. "I did not start this boycott. I was asked by you to serve as your spokesman. I want it known the length and breadth of this land that if I am stopped, this movement will not stop, for what we are doing is right and just! God is with us and is on our side. Go home to your families and know that all of us are in the hands of God!"

Now Commissioner Sellers addressed the group. "I do not condone such acts of violence as this, and I will certainly do everything in my power to bring the guilty parties to trial. Though I do not agree with you in your belief, I will do all in my power to protect you against such acts as these." He also promised to provide police protection for the King family.

Following Mr. Sellers was Mayor Gayle, who gave his sanction to the commissioner's promise. "I am for law and order, and the entire white community is for law and order. None of us condones or believes in these sorts of acts in any way. I am going to work, with my last breath if necessary, to find the guilty parties. We ask the entire community to cooperate with us in apprehending the guilty ones."

County Sheriff Mac Sim Butler was there aiding in the investigation. He added, "I am opposed to such acts of violence and will furnish men and equipment, or anything within my power, to help find the guilty parties."

An *Advertiser* photographer took pictures of the city administrators addressing the huge gathering.

To some of the members of the crowd, the officials' statements had seemed empty. Critics said that there had been no feeling in

Mayor Gayle's words, or in his voice. Many of the hundreds of people now surrounding Dr. King's home were angry, and they showed it. Some were crying; some were swearing and threatening revenge; some were praying; some were just standing there and staring into space. They were suspicious of the three city commissioners, of the large crowds who assembled so quickly, of every unfamiliar face in those crowds. In their helplessness, the followers of Dr. King needed somebody to blame, to accuse, to cast their suspicions on. And they stood there, hundreds of them!

Dr. King asked the crowds to go home, to sleep calmly, not to worry. And the crowds, which had refused to move at the police's insistence, moved away as a great surge of water rolls quietly, calmly, obediently downstream.

Ten years ago these same people would have been frightened beyond words at the bombing. But these new black Americans were not afraid. They were not afraid of the police, or of the city commissioners, or of physical harm. They had defiantly stood there, throughout the pleadings of police officers that they leave, and moved only when Dr. King, assuring them that he and his family were safe, bade them move.

The City Commission offered a reward of $500 for "capture and conviction of the guilty ones." The White Citizens Council offered a similar award. But no one was ever apprehended. Until this day, however, the black citizens of Montgomery believe that opponents of the boycott were determined to stop it at any cost.

7

The Legal Battle

Going to Court

In the meantime, Attorney Fred D. Gray had been entertaining visitors. Many black people had approached him about the possibility of a suit to restrain the police force from further intimidations of them. The police, they said, were using their authority as officers of the law to try to force black riders to start riding buses again. Still others, who had tired of walking yet saw no immediate solution to the bus problem, had asked Gray and his colleagues to represent them in a suit against the commissioners and against the segregation laws themselves.

Up until late January, black people had not been making a real effort to abolish segregation on city transportation lines, but only to secure a satisfactory seating arrangement *under* the segregation laws. And until now no one had brought a case against the City of Montgomery for the purpose of integrating the buses, or any other transportation facility. But now people had gotten tired; had gained more courage; had sworn to break down all segregation in the area of travel. Now they felt they had no choice! The City Commission had seen to that.

At the request of clients, attorneys had looked into the matter but had hesitated, since they expected, because of the present situation in the city, some case involving the integration issue to be brought before the courts. Lawyers also had hesitated to file the cases because of fear of reprisals they felt the filing would evoke, since such a suit would undoubtedly be brought by black people against white people. The lawyers spent days pondering. One attorney warned his clients of threats, intimidations, disturbing telephone calls, and the like, and insisted that the potential plaintiffs "be quite sure that you know what you are doing." The plaintiffs had waited a few days, and the attorneys waited, too.

It has already been mentioned that during this time, a group of young black lawyers were coming to the front line of recognition. These young men, all highly trained and ambitious, inspired by faith in the prospect of a new day for black Americans, united as a team to serve as lawyers for boycotters. These lawyers were from Montgomery and Birmingham. Working with them was Clifford Durr, a brilliant white lawyer who has already been mentioned in these pages. The lawyers burned the midnight oil many nights preparing their case, for they knew that the lawyers for the City of Montgomery would be merciless in their efforts to defeat them. And the black lawyers could not afford to be defeated; the stakes were too high. Innocent people—the boycotters—literally would be destroyed if the case were lost. The lawyers *had* to win the case!

Then Dr. King's home was bombed. That was it! On Tuesday, January 31, 1956, Fred Gray was authorized by five of his clients to file the suit. Gray, assisted by attorneys Charles Langford, Clifford Durr, and other lawyers, worked all Tuesday and Tuesday night preparing the legal documents. By 11 A.M. on Wednesday, February 1, the papers were ready to be filed in the U.S. District Court. This case was designed to integrate all transportation in the city of Montgomery.

The plaintiffs in the case were Misses Claudette Colvin and Mary Louise Smith, both teenagers who had been arrested and convicted in connection with bus mishaps (they were spoken for by their fathers, Mr. Q. P. Colvin and Mr. Frank Smith); Mrs. Jeannetta Reese, a domestic who had an invalid husband; Mrs. Aurelia Browder; and Mrs. Susie McDonald. All of these women had suffered on the buses.

Mrs. Browder, a tall, heavy-set mother of six children, was a seamstress. As a widow, she had the responsibility of providing for her children by herself. And she did an admirable job. She was a good mother and citizen, well-read, highly intelligent, fearless. She had to ride the bus and she tried to follow the law in taking a seat on the bus. But she took no foolishness from drivers. If a driver tried to get rough with her, she stopped it quickly. She was not afraid to go to court to settle problems, for she felt that that was what they were there for. She never ran away from any problem, but instead found ways of solving it.

Mrs. McDonald, a widow and housekeeper for her son, was a very fair black lady. Her blue eyes, very white skin, very straight, light tan hair, often misled people to believe that she was white. It angered her to be mistaken in that sense, and she spoke out in her own behalf, explaining that she was a "member of the darker race." When a driver cautioned her not to sit in areas on the bus reserved for blacks, she enjoyed getting him straightened out. Then she would laugh at him, while he fumed over his mistake. Mrs. McDonald, like Mrs. Browder, was a courageous woman, fearless, and a fighter for the rights of every human, no matter the race or color. Since she was so often mistaken for a member of the white race, she would laughingly say, "race is the accident of birth."

The defendants named in the suit were Mayor W. A. Gayle, Commissioner Clyde Sellers, and Commissioner Frank Parks, charged individually and collectively as members of the Board of Commissioners of the City of Montgomery; Police Chief Goodwyn J. Ruppenthal, individually and as chief of police; the Montgomery City Lines, Inc.; and Mr. James F. Blake and Mr. Robert Cleere, bus drivers at the time of the arrests of Claudette Colvin and Mrs. Rosa Parks.

According to the *Advertiser*, the suit, filed for the plaintiffs and all other black citizens similar situated, asked:

1. That a three-judge court order a speedy hearing and enter a temporary and permanent injunction to enjoin and restrain each defendant (mayor, commissioners, police department) from enforcing laws that would compel black citizens by force, threats, violence, intimidation, or harassment, to use facilities provided by the Montgomery City Lines.

2. That the courts declare, define, and give judgment on the legal rights of the parties in relationship to the subject matter of the controversy, and declare the city segregation laws (Section 301, Title, 48, Code of Alabama 1940, and Section 10–11 of the Code of the City of Montgomery 1952, which ordered bus segregation) unconstitutional, null, and void.
3. That a temporary and permanent injunction be issued, ordering all defendants or their agents or employees from taking acts to prevent, by force, threats, violence, intimidation, or harassment, the plaintiffs or other Negro citizens from using privately provided transportation.

In his *Advertiser* editorial that day, Editor Grover C. Hall wrote, "We have already begun to see what the late Justice Robert H. Jackson meant when he said of the segregation problem, 'I foresee a generation of litigation!'"

The Violence Continues

That night the home of Mr. E. D. Nixon was bombed. The afternoon before the bombing, a snaggle-toothed, tobacco-chewing, poorly dressed white man walked down Clinton Street, on which Mr. Nixon lived, inquiring which house the Negro activist lived in. Those who talked with the man felt that he might have been locating the house for the guilty ones. This was the second bombing of boycotters' homes, with no injuries and no arrests.

In some ways, however, the filing of the suit seemed to have the effect of magic! For a short time all intimidations stopped. As in the lull before the storm, things grew quiet. No longer did the downtown parking lot swim with policemen. No longer did bus drivers stop their empty buses and get out quickly to scribble down license numbers of black drivers' cars as they stopped to pick up passengers along the way. Policemen even stopped going to churches in the early morning hours to rout domestics as they waited at the dispatch stations—previously a common occurrence at Bethel, Day Street, and Holt Street Churches. At one time Reverend H. H. Hubbard, pastor at Bethel, had told the law officers that they had no right to trespass upon church property.

The tension seemed to lessen, and things looked brighter. Even the news from the Tuscaloosa area was heartening. On February 1, Miss Authurine Lucy began attending classes at the University of Alabama. Not allowed to live in the dormitory with other students, Miss Lucy was commuting from Birmingham, a distance of fifty-eight miles each way. Things were not as quiet as they could have been, for crosses had been burned and small demonstrations held among students and townfolk, but the Negro coed *was* in school. That was something! Everyone expected the demonstrations to be brought under control in a few days.

Nevertheless, terrorizing by policemen, or men dressed as police officers, continued. Reverend Abernathy became a target, as did the MIA financial secretary, Mrs. Dungee, and many other boycotters. Demolition of automobiles parked in front of houses; spraying yards to destroy beautiful flowers; throwing paint on homes, necessitating new paint jobs; throwing nails in paths of automobiles, causing the tires to puncture; even throwing human manure on porches were among the things black civilians accused white policemen of doing.

I too became a target of police, or people dressed in police regalia. Although I had tried to keep a low profile, I was president of the WPC and a member of the MIA Executive Board, had served on most of the key committees, and edited the *MIA Newsletter.* One night I and two of my friends, man and wife, who often sat with me until bedtime, were chatting in my living room. Two policemen in a squad car rode past; one got out, threw a big stone through my picture window, then walked back to the car, and got in. Unhurriedly, the two rode away. Glass scattered everywhere, and we three fell to the floor and lay there until the car had moved on. Afterward we had to walk very cautiously to keep from being cut. The large picture window was completely broken out, and we had to pick up the large pieces before we could sweep up the small ones. Before my friends left, the husband got some wide planks from his yard and boarded up that window to keep out the wind and cold. It stayed boarded up for the duration of the boycott.

In the meantime, my friends had gotten in their car and driven down to city hall to report the attack, and to bear witness to it. They carried with them the squad car number and license plate number, which another neighbor had been able to get before the officers drove away. They made their report to the officer in charge, gave him the stone, wrapped in tissue to preserve any fingerprints, and waited for him to speak. Another officer nearby got up, walked to the desk where the two stood, and asked, "Do y'all want to live?" The neighbors immediately replied that they did. "Well, then, y'all go home where y'all belong; keep your mouths shut; and tend to yo' business."

Returning, my friends recounted to other neighbors the story of the attack as they had seen it, expressed their regrets to me, and went home, badly shaken. They never mentioned the experience again.

Two weeks later about 2 A.M., my neighbors next door, good friends, knocked on my door and reported that two men in police uniform had scattered acid all over the top, sides, and hood of my car. The car had been parked under the carport at the side of the house. The neighbors had heard the noise, peeped out their window, and witnessed the acid attack.

By morning, holes, some as large as silver dollars, were all over the top, fenders, and hood. Apologetically, the neighbor said that he had to protect his family and would not testify that he had witnessed the evil deed. I did not ask him to do so, nor would I have, for I would not have wanted them to become targets for attack, too.

I kept that car, a Chrysler, until 1960, after I had resigned from Alabama State. It had become the most beautiful car in the world to me. I turned it in for a new one only when I moved to California, for I did not think the Chrysler would hold up through the deserts I had to cross.

After those attacks, Governor Folsom ordered state officers to keep an eye on the homes of boycott leaders. But for some strange reason I had never been afraid! When my picture window was broken out by the police, I was more angry than afraid, because I had the bill to pay. Then, too, friends sat with me each night until midnight, so I had no reason to be afraid of the police, just angry that they had deliberately attempted to destroy my home. Still, it meant something to me that Governor Folsom had acted to protect us. For the first time in months I was able to retire before midnight and arise the next morning rested and ready to go to my classes. I felt safe now, relaxed; I could sleep, too. Then those many friends who had taken turns sitting with me until after twelve each night could stay home and get the rest they needed. And most of all, I knew now that somebody cared!

A few days after Fred Gray filed the suit in federal court contesting the constitutionality of segregation on city buses, his draft board changed Gray's classification from 4-D to 1-A. He had been put in Class 4-D because of his ministerial status. In addition to being a lawyer, Gray was a trained, ordained minister of the gospel and often served in the church. For this reason he had been exempted from the draft.

Whether the filing of the federal suit had any influence upon the draft board or not, no one can say for sure. However, the case was filed on February 1, 1956. Soon after Gray was notified to appear before the draft board on February 7. It was at that meeting that he was reclassified 1-A. Gray appealed the case. In the end, his reclassification came to naught. Although he was 1-A, he was never inducted into the service.

The Grand Jury Investigation

In mid-February, Judge Eugene Carter asked the grand jury to investigate the Negro bus boycott, for some whites were demanding an investigation.

The grand jury is an independent judicial investigative body called by authorities to hear complaints concerning the commission of crimes and to inquire by aid of testimony whether *prima facie* evidence exists for making accusations or indictments. A grand jury functions not only to determine whether persons accused of crime shall be indicted and therefore tried, but also to inquire into such matters relating to crime as may be confided to it by a court, or which may come to its knowledge in other ways. According to press reports, Judge Carter called the investigative group in Montgomery "the grand inquisitorial body."

At that time, in 1956, Alabama had a law concerning boycotts (State Code, Title 14, Section 54). Although many felt that the law might be unconstitutional, since an adjoining section forbidding labor union picketing had been declared so, the law was still on the books. It read:

> Two or more persons who, without a just cause or legal excuse for so doing, enter into any combination, conspiracy, agreement, arrangement, or understanding for the purpose of hindering, delaying, or preventing any other persons, firms, corporations, or association of persons from carrying on any lawful business, shall be guilty of a misdemeanor. [Furthermore,] any person, firm, corporation or association of persons who prints or circulates any notice of boycott, boycott cards, stickers, dodgers, or unfair lists, publishing or declaring that a boycott or ban exists or has existed or is contemplated against any person, firm, corporation or association of persons doing a lawful business, shall be guilty of a misdemeanor.

It was under this provision that the boycotters were considered to have engaged in illegal activity.

The Montgomery County Grand Jury was composed of eighteen people of various professions and stations in life, twelve of whom had to be in agreement before indictments could be made. In prosecution against Negroes, a black person had to be on the grand jury, or else a higher court might throw out the indictment on the grounds that Negroes were systematically excluded from jury service. To comply with the law, then, at least one Negro had to be included. In this case, the black was E. T. Sinclair, a waiter at the white Montgomery Country Club.

Almost simultaneously, one of the plaintiffs in the federal suit, Mrs. Jeannetta Reese, withdrew her name from the suit. After a period in Mayor Gayle's office, in the presence of the city commissioners and newsmen, she asked that her name be stricken from the list of plaintiffs. She declared that she had not known what she was signing and that she had been intimidated by heavy pressure. She also stated that her husband was ill at home, and that she was afraid of physical harm to herself and her household. Later the frightened woman said privately that she *had* known what she was signing, but wanted to withdraw her name because she could not stand the pressure.

As a result of Mrs. Reese's testimony before the grand jury and her withdrawal from the federal suit, Fred Gray was indicted by the grand jury on the charge that he was representing clients without authority. He was arrested, fingerprinted, numbered, and photographed. If convicted, he could be disbarred from further law practice and fined heavily besides.

Special police guarded the Reese home after this. From six in the evening until six in the morning, uniformed police protected the woman's house from attack or harassment.

Shadows darkened as the grand jury began to subpoena black leaders for investigation. First to be called were the plaintiffs of the suit. Then the gasoline station operators, some ministers, attorney Langford, the taxi drivers who had cooperated in the boycott, and the MIA financial and recording secretaries. Photostatic copies of checks written on the MIA checking account at the Alabama National Bank in Montgomery appeared as evidence. I was not subpoenaed and never attended a single hearing.

When word circulated that the grand jury had been authorized to "arrest leaders of the boycott" and insinuated that large sums were being paid to individuals as part of the boycott effort, none of the boycotters were upset. They knew that every penny received by the MIA had been freely given to it by the people, and they had complete faith in the honesty of the leaders they had chosen. That faith was justified, for during the entire period of the boycott, no serious question ever arose concerning any MIA officer's honesty in dealing with money.

Fred Gray's indictment, the grand jury's subpoenaing of dozens of black citizens, and the investigation of MIA records all pointed toward the likelihood of further indictments. Black people were getting more tense and began to show it. They did not know what to expect from the grand jury. They expected mass arrests, because the boycott had been staged not by a few people, but by fifty thousand black people. Still, everybody couldn't be arrested, for there were not enough jails to hold them all. But after two weeks of interrogation, the waiting for the grand jury's report and indictments, the uncertainty, the suspense—these were nerve-wracking.

On Friday night, February 10, some 15,000 whites, among

them White Citizens Council members and sympathizers, were expected to meet at the coliseum to hear United States Senator James O. Eastland speak. The national figure from Mississippi had been labeled the spokesman for the South on the segregation question. Also news had circulated that the wcc would congregate in mass to hear him, and that other followers from all around the area would be on the scene for the entire time.

Black people all over Montgomery had passed the word along for blacks to get off the streets early and relax at home that night. Police had given orders for Negro nightclubs to close up, as they had done on the night that Dr. King's home was bombed.

As predicted, small-town white people arrived from every section of Alabama for the event. An estimated 11,000 whites packed the coliseum. The senator was greeted by the city commissioners, who shared the platform with him. According to the *Advertiser,* the speaker made reference only to "the uprising at the University of Alabama" and "completely sidestepped the Montgomery bus boycott." Evidently many had gone there to hear the senator discuss the immediate problems at hand—the university case and, by all means, the bus boycott. When he did not, "crowds began to move toward the exits in increasing numbers, so much so that the pro-segregationist had to delete the last six pages of his prepared address."

The next day a handbill, fashioned after the Declaration of Independence and supposedly circulated at the coliseum the night before, fell into the hands of a maid emptying a wastepaper basket. During the day an identical copy was given to a black man by his white co-worker. Another one came through a white man whose sole support came from black people. Who circulated these, or how they were circulated, is not known.

Meetings with the Men of Montgomery

At this time the Men of Montgomery (MOM), an organization of some thirty-seven white businessmen, were seeking to meet with leaders of the boycotting group, to try to bring about an end to the bus boycott. Through the efforts of Reverend Thrasher, one of the three persons who had brought the MIA and white officials together earlier, seven of us (Dr. King, Reverend Abernathy, Dr. Moses W. Jones, Reverend Hubbard, Reverend A. W. Wilson, Professor J. E. Pierce, and me) met with seven of them to discuss ways of calling off the protest. No promises were made at that time, but the Men of Montgomery were easy to talk with. There was hope for a settlement.

On Monday, February 13, the same Negro delegation met with the Men of Montgomery for the second time to discuss ending the boycott. Thirty-seven MOM members were led by representatives who spoke in this meeting: Mr. Joe Bear, chairman of the Bear Lumber Company; Mr. C. T. Fitzpatrick, vice president of the Empire Rouse Company and former president of the Chamber of Commerce; Mr. R. H. McCrory, president of Montgomery Fair Department Store; Mr. Winton Blount of the Blount Construction Company; Mr. Lamar Burford of Burford Machinery; and Mr. Frank Tennille, president of the Tennille Furniture Company.

Both groups made a sincere, earnest effort to reach a solution. This time the MOM presented a set of proposals, which they asked the MIA to consider approving. The trouble was that the proposals they were offering were the same ones that had been offered and rejected before!

It was evident now that blacks would never return to the public carriers except on an integrated basis. The system now in use was giving them transportation back and forth, so black riders knew that they could afford to wait. Black people knew, too, that some white riders were doing without transportation. They felt that eventually the City would have to give in and integrate those buses, as other southern cities had done.

That meeting adjourned, and the black group promised to carry the proposals back to the MIA Executive Board and to a mass meeting for a vote, knowing well that they would be turned down. They were! On Thursday morning, February 16, at the MIA Executive Board's regular meeting, the proposals were rejected.

Before the MIA representatives met with the MOM for one last time, we requested one more interview with Mr. Bagley. We questioned the possibility of reducing the reserved seats to five; of reducing the increased bus fare to what it had been prior to the boy-cott; of black drivers on predominantly black passenger buses. Mr. Bagley listened intently to our requests. Then he stated that he would ask Mr. Totten to come from Chicago to Montgomery once more, for the purpose of answering our questions and clarifying any other thing necessary to end the boycott.

During the waiting period, the committee held its third and final meeting with the MOM. At this third meeting, the only differ-ence between the new proposals and the first ones presented by the MOM was this:

> #6(b): Whenever the condition exists that there is no possibility of any additional white passengers boarding the bus, or any colored passengers as the case may be, in that event the bus operator shall assign such seats as may be required in the reserved section.
>
> #6(c): All passengers shall enter the front door of the bus. [A clause about packages in one's arms causing one to have to get on at the back was deleted.]
>
> #7: Emergency bus fares now existing will remain in effect for a temporary time only. The fare will return to ten cents at such time as sufficient patronage permits the bus company to operate under the schedule adopted by the City Commission.

Most importantly, however, the MOM could not accept the idea of re-serving only five seats for white riders; there had to be ten seats.

Mr. Totten flew down from Chicago and conferred with the City Commission, but not with the Negro group. Thus, there was no reply to our requests for (1) fare reduction; (2) employment for black drivers; and (3) reserving five seats rather than ten for whites. There was nothing for our committee to do but present the MOM proposals to the masses of blacks.

Approximately five thousand people jammed the church that Monday night, February 20, to hear those final proposals. The main auditorium, the basement, and outside were crowded with people who waited skeptically for the reading of this very last offer. The people had suffered for so long, waited so long for some kind of agreement, that there was no predicting what their reaction would be when they heard what was brought back to them. Thus far, dignity and calm had dominated their spirit and personalities, but people were tired and impatient. Such a letdown after their anxious anticipation could prove embarrassing to our cause. The ministers heretofore had maintained good control, but they preferred not to have newsmen on hand that night. Thus, newsmen had been barred from this meeting.

Reverend Abernathy read the proposals as presented and asked the congregation to vote on them. Two people who voted "Yes" were booed and jeered unmercifully by the congregation.

Since they were not admitted to the meeting, reporters had been waiting outside for the results of the mass vote on the proposal. They were somewhat surprised when told that the proposals had been rejected. Television stations broadcast the report that night, and wire services carried it over the country. The Tuesday morning newspaper headlines stirred public interest to a higher pitch, with the same papers hinting that mass arrests would follow the grand jury's final report that same day, February 21.

8

Grand Jury Report, Arrests, Trial, and Verdict

The Grand Jury Report

On Tuesday, February 21, in the second week of the investigation into the bus protest, the grand jury completed its work and gave its final report to the courts. Tuesday afternoon's newspapers reported the action of the jury. The boycott was judged illegal, and 115 black boycott leaders were to be arrested by Wednesday morning. No whites were indicted.

In the same report, the grand jury asked the city commissioners to forbid the sale of knives, guns, pistols, and any ammunition or weapons anywhere in the city, and also to adopt an ordinance requesting every city resident who owned a pistol to register it. Apparently the City did not carry out these recommendations, or if it did so, there was little or no publicity about it.

The news of the grand jury action came over the radio and television on the day of the announcement. After that the newspapers carried in detail all the facts in the case. However, the boycotters had been expecting the announcement, and it seemed to allay the fears of those blacks who tended to be nervous, for 115 people could not possibly get lonely or afraid in jail together. Already lawyers had been notified to take care of all boycotters, and none of us expected to remain in jail even overnight. If we had to, the large numbers would overcome the fears to be experienced, for few of us had ever been in jail before.

We just took the news as a joke, a pretense, an excitement for the moment. We just did not look beyond to anything else. Negroes laughed, determined to stand their ground. They were defiant, willing to go to jail, ready to let Americans and the world know that they could not and would not take any more. One thing we knew. No power on earth could force fifty thousand people back to the buses. Black people were now ready to fight in the courts, even to die, for justice and freedom. Death could not possibly be worse than what Montgomery's black citizens were experiencing at this time; even hell, as they envisioned it, could be no worse!

The Arrests

The next morning, Wednesday, February 22, 1956, the mass arrests ordered by the grand jury began. The leading ministers were picked up first. They were fingerprinted, photographed, given case numbers, and released when they made bond. When Dr. King, Reverend Abernathy, and other ministers were arrested and taken to jail, they asked for the list of names of persons to be arrested, so they could notify people on the list to come to the courthouse. The arresting officers obliged them, for they were delighted that the rest of us would come down on our own. We were grateful as well, for as fast as we could, we notified those persons who had been indicted, and organized groups to drive to the courthouse and give themselves up. Boycotters picked up other friends who were going to be arrested and carried them along. This saved the police and the City quite some effort, for, instead of the police having to pick everyone up, most of the remaining 115 persons went down on their own and did not wait for the free ride to county jail.

Dr. King called me to get Mrs. West, who was in her seventies, and to come down. I responded quickly, so I would not be arrested at the college where I taught. Mr. Robert Nesbitt, Mr. Elisa James, and Mr. Alfonso Campbell did not want Mrs. West and me, the leaders, to go down and be arrested by ourselves, and so they came for us. However, we were not afraid or worried, for we knew that we had done nothing to be worried about. We were met at the jail by the cheerful ministers who gave us words of encouragement as we were ushered into the dark, dingy rooms of the county courthouse. As fast as we were arrested, our lawyers were there to bond us out. After fingerprinting and the other necessary procedures, we were released.

If there was any nervousness or uneasiness, it was on the part of the whites who worked there, not the blacks being arrested. Reverend E. N. French, pastor of Hilliard Chapel Church, declared that the officer taking fingerprints was so nervous that he could not maneuver very well. When Reverend French saw how it was supposed to be done, he told the nervous officer to allow *him* to fingerprint himself, and he did.

After we were fingerprinted, thumb included, by the city detectives, some of the officers began to joke with us. They seemed anxious to put us women at ease—to allay our fears and make the ordeal less grueling. They asked about Alabama State College, the enrollment, Dr. Trenholm. One of them, a very young officer, lamented the fact that he had not finished college. Mrs. West assured him that, to judge by the competent manner in which he was processing the boycotters, he did not need a degree. We all laughed at that, especially the officer, who beamed, pleased with the compliment. The other officers laughed, too. The interchange was good for all of us, and we felt wonderful, relaxed, at peace with ourselves and with the friendly officers who had processed our arrest and "booking." We were not angry at policemen, for now we did not have to wait in suspense anymore. Each day we had expected to be arrested. Now we did not have to wait any longer. The suspense was over!

Now we moved on to the next table, where we were numbered (my number was 7042) and our pictures taken with huge numbers looped around our necks like convicts. Information such as age, height, weight, date and place of birth, color of eyes, color of hair, teeth markings, place of employment, marital status, and next of kin was recorded by the identification officer. He also wanted to know if we had ever been arrested before, and if so, for what? None of us had.

To keep up morale, Mrs. West and I joked with each other and kept up a subdued conversation among ourselves and others. All of a sudden, the identification officer yelled, "Shut up the noise!" We continued our aimless chatter, though in more subdued tones. He yelled again, "Shut up, or I will throw you out of here!" Since we would have relished being put out, we chuckled and kept on talking, though very, very softly.

When the officer had finished getting the information he needed, he said to me, "Get out of here! You have too much mouth!" I informed him that I wanted to wait for my elderly friend, Mrs. West, who was not too well and needed to have someone near in the event she became ill.

"Get out of here," he repeated, "before I put you in this jail where nobody will ever be able to get you out." He stared at me angrily. Then he gave me a slight push, to start me on to the next room where bonds were being made. The "push" did not hurt me physically, but it wounded my pride, for others waiting to be processed had seen it and were laughing among themselves.

"Thank you so much," I said to the officer, smiling. My expression seemed to madden him.

"Don't thank me," he snapped. "Thank the Lord you are still living!" His eyes were like daggers.

"Well, thank the Lord and all his saints, then," I replied. A second officer attempted to usher me toward the next room, apparently to help me avoid an unpleasant scene with the first man. However, I did not move. I was certainly nervous, for this was the first time I had ever been inside a jail, much less under arrest. But I also resented the manner in which that first officer had spoken to me, and the tone of his voice as he did so. Something constrained me to stand there and to speak again to that officer. Something about his facial expression had bothered me, and I could *feel* his eyes still upon me. Slowly I turned around and looked at him. He had not moved, nor had he begun to process the next arrested boycotter. He stood there, staring at me, his eyes glaring contemptuously. For a second I stood there, too, looking into those pale blue eyes. As I did I could feel the hate, the bitterness, the helpless anger that were consuming that middle-aged white man. I felt that he was being devoured by his racial hatred. A feeling of sorrow and pity for that man inundated me. I felt like crying. Mentally I forgave him for pushing me and breathed a silent prayer that he would find peace within himself. Words seemed to flood my thoughts, and without conscious effort they poured from my lips with all the sincerity I possessed: "Sir," I said, "I did not mean to give you a hard time. Please try to have a good day."

His eyes ceased staring at me and suddenly focused on the floor. I smiled at him, an honest, sincere smile, and somehow I had the feeling that he had lifted his eyes and smiled back. This time, feeling much better, I entered the section where bonds were being made, and soon I was released.

When a person gets arrested, the first thing he does is to get a bondsman to go "on his bond." That means that, if the bondsman is a man of wealth, all he has to do is to write his signature, stating that he will be responsible for the client until the case goes to court. Then, if that person skips bail, the bondsman has to pay that bill. On the other hand, if the person is honest and honorable, he will see the case through and the bondsman is only out his time. The client has to pay a fee for this help. Many bondsmen make their money doing such.

In our case, nobody charged us any fees. The bondsmen were friends and accommodated all of us because of that friendship. Our boycotting helped them, too, for it broke up the complete disrespect and disregard for black Americans that held sway during the period under consideration.

The bonds were $300 each. Since the day was far spent, all banks were closed. If cash had been required, many arrested people would have had to stay in jail all night, until banks opened the next day. A few could have gotten out, for this amount of money is often kept in homes for emergencies. A few would have gotten out through the efforts of friends who brought cash to aid them until the banks opened the next day. Also, there were several white professional bondsmen in waiting who could have made those thirty dollars per person, but they were not needed.

No cash money had to be posted, luckily, for Negro property owners, and several white men, too, came rushing down to do bonds. The *Advertiser* reported, "Early in the morning, several Negroes appeared at the jail ready to sign bonds for the arrested Negroes. They did sign the bonds—but as the indictment warrants were issued, it was discovered some of those signing bonds were to be arrested themselves on the boycotting charges. After that, Sheriff Mac Sim Butler ordered the indictment list be checked before a person could sign a bond."

One report stated that Mr. Dungee Caffey, a black businessman, had put up the money for our release and that he had informed Fred Gray that he would sign as many bonds as were needed. Another report was rampant that a very wealthy white man had put up the guarantee necessary for our release. We learned later that Mr. Aubrey Williams, a humanitarian white gentleman, publisher of the *Southern Farmer* and former director of the National Youth Administration, had been there to go on bonds for arrested black citizens if they needed him to. Very soon, then, all MIA persons were out on bail.

According to the *Advertiser,* "the arrest list caused many complications. Addresses weren't always correct. Names were wrong in some instances. The deputies struggled with the city directory and questioned the arrested parties." Rufus Lewis voluntarily appeared for arrest. Although his name did appear on a four-page list of those indicted, later it was discovered that he had not actually been indicted. After the error was discovered, he was released.

In the end, after errors and duplications were corrected, only 89 of the 115 indicted were actually arrested. As the paper stated, "The files of those arrested showed 90 percent were Alabama-born Negroes. Their birth places for the most part were small Alabama towns. Most were born on farms. The majority were in the 35 to 50 age bracket. None were under 23." The oldest person arrested was Dr. M. C. Cleveland, pastor of the Day Street Baptist Church. He commented, "This is the first time I have ever been arrested for anything in 72 years. This is a new experience but I suppose at my age you are used to new experiences."

As has been stated, when the boycott began, people everywhere sent funds to support it. But following the arrests, the MIA received thousands of dollars from churches, various organizations, and individuals to help pay court fees and to employ good lawyers for the indicted victims. Such money was needed, for at the height of the carpool, MIA expenses ran into thousands of dollars. The boycott lasted a year. During the arrests and trials, lawyers had to be paid. We had half a dozen lawyers, white and black, working for us, some periodically, others regularly. Possibly six months of regular payments ensued. There was always a need for funds.

The first mass meeting to be held following the wholesale arrests was at the First Baptist Church. The historic place was jammed to capacity. Thousands of people had gathered since three o'clock in the afternoon. Long before seven o'clock, there was no room upstairs or down; the crowds sang and prayed to Almighty God for four hours, until the ministers came in and took over at the hour of seven. Nobody got tired.

The high point of the evening came when Reverend Abernathy requested that "race-loving blacks would not turn a key in the switch, nor touch a starter, nor take a cab, but would walk everywhere that Friday, so that those who walked would know that others walked with them."

The masses readily took up the spirit and set Friday aside as a Pilgrim-Prayer Day. Before the meeting adjourned, thousands had agreed to park their cars on Friday and walk to the courthouse. Only doctors, ambulances, and hearses were to operate by motorized force. All others would operate on human energy.

The Arraignments

The arraignments for trial of those indicted by the grand jury were set for 9:30 Friday morning, February 24. Long lines of walking pilgrims headed in the direction of the Montgomery County courthouse in a drizzling rain. The indicted persons, along with some

200 sympathizers, filed through the courthouse doors and up the narrow flight of steps, at the top of which stood reporters with cameras clicking as the weary ones, who had walked to town in observance of Pilgrim-Prayer Day, ascended. As we entered, our names were checked on a list by an officer posted at the door. All 89 were seated, and those not indicted were allowed to enter and take an empty seat. Since no one was allowed to stand, the rest of the crowd was turned back. These either left or waited outside until they were rejoined by those on trial.

Those in charge seemed very nervous, which may have accounted for the long delay. When a white freelance cameraman came to the door of the courtroom, snapped a picture, and left hurriedly, a judge shouted for someone to "Catch that man!" After a quick pause, he added, "And bring him back!" Soon the fellow, escorted by policemen, came in and stood before the judge.

"Were you commanded to take *no* pictures in the courtroom?" the judge asked the trembling figure angrily.

"I was not inside the courtroom, sir," the man replied nervously. "I stood outside! An officer gave me permission to come to the door."

"Who gave him permission to come to the door?" queried the judge of the officers. He was told that someone had let him through.

"You are excused this time," His Honor answered, "but don't try it again, or you'll go to jail!" The relieved man walked out smiling, his picture safe in his camera.

But the awkward nervousness continued. Black boycotters laughed and carried on subdued conversations, as calm and relaxed as could be. If they were not calm internally, they managed to conceal it. Several times laughter penetrated the courtroom as errors and duplications in the indictment were acknowledged and declared nolle prosequi. The judge stated, "Laughter is not permitted in the courtroom, but since the occasion warrants it, it will be permitted this time."

After monotonous hours, the process was finished. Dr. King's case was set for trial in advance of all the others and given a trial date. The crowds of those indicted and their sympathizers filed out of the courtroom and marched in quiet groups to Dexter Avenue Baptist Church, where a forty-five-minute spiritual meeting was held. Songs were sung, and prayers were prayed by four ministers who stood while the congregation sat with bowed heads.

The first prayer asked God to give courage, to vanquish fear, to help all darker people to "stand together or to go down together." Reverend J. W. Bonner's petition to the Almighty acknowledged that "we are black, but God made us black." The plea reminded me of King Solomon's confession, "I am black, but comely!" Reverend Bonner asked for "overcoming faith." He said that the group was more determined and asked God's guidance in the right direction. "If we are wrong, God, whisper it to us, and we will turn back right now," pleaded the minister, "but if we are right, stay nearby."

Reverend B. D. Lambert's prayer expressed faith, for he saw God's hand in the unique experiences of the boycott. He recalled the "martyred, persecuted men of old who had fought for right" and asked God to help dark Americans to bear their burdens in the fight for justice.

Dr. King, in a brief speech, stated: "Up to the time of Christ, the cross was a symbol of crime. Since that time it has become a symbol of victory, faith, and love!" Comparing the cross with the jail, Dr. King declared, "The Montgomery County Jail has taken on a different meaning for black people. It is a symbol portraying a struggle for justice, a fight for rights."

Agreeing with Dr. King, Reverend M. W. Whitt of Harmony Street Baptist Church in Birmingham said that "no jail is more blessed, no courtroom more honored, because a host of God's children has been there." As the group left the church, we sang a song set to the tune of "Give Me That Old Time Religion."

Certainly the Spirit from above must have been among the crowd, for people were mentally, spiritually, psychologically serene inside. Even I, always demanding proof for statements, felt a special peace within myself. A quiet calm seemed to invade and relax me. At the very beginning of the movement, I had put myself in the hands of the unseen power from above, and since then there had been no turning back. After that I never thought of myself, my job, my future. My thoughts were in the *now!* I believe all the people felt the same way.

Judge Carter's original request that the grand jury investigate the bus boycott, and the talk of possible indictments had stirred concern and protest not only on the local level, but also nationally. People could not help wondering what the grand jury would do about economic pressure directed against whites by Negroes. Then, in the wake of the indictments, scores of newspaper, television, and radio personnel from all over the U.S. and elsewhere poured into Montgomery. They flooded the local press office, the City Commission, and the homes of the boycotters, seeking any news at all.

News stories about the indictments made front-page headlines in newspapers all over the country. If the City Commission earlier had been deluged with congratulations on their stand against the movement, now there were as many or more congratulations to black people for the movement!

Newspapers at home and abroad questioned the bombings, the mass arrests, the reasons for bus segregation in the first place. Why did *where* one sat on a bus make such a difference, anyway? How could sitting beside black people be so contaminating to whites, when blacks kept their homes, nursed their babies, prepared their meals? It was too incredible to reason out! One northern journalist had thought that Shakespeare's phrase, "much ado about nothing," described the Montgomery situation perfectly. In the East, North, and West, and in some cities in the South, seating on public vehicles was integrated. Why not in Montgomery?

Now, as we waited for the trials to begin, newspaper reporters asked how the prosecution could prove its accusations that boycotters' main purpose was to put the bus company out of business. What if trials were held and cases dismissed for lack of proof? What if they showed that the "intent" of the boycotters was not to destroy the company but to secure equality of opportunity as bus riders?

Everybody kept close tabs on radio, television, and newspapers to see how the trials would be conducted—that is, whether the other cases following Dr. King's would be heard as a group or individually. We were told by our lawyers that if Dr. King was found guilty, the case would be appealed to a federal court, and with a thorough investigation, all of the arrested persons would be exonerated. But boycotters grew more nervous as each day passed and no announcement was forthcoming.

Dr. King's Trial

Finally the day of Dr. King's trial arrived. What if Dr. King were found guilty? Then would all the other boycotters be found guilty?

The strongest evidence in favor of the boycotters was that *they had simply stopped riding the buses*. They had stopped of their own free will, because they chose not to ride them anymore. There was no law against that! There had been no attacks against the buses or the drivers. Black people had simply *stopped riding*. But what would be the outcome if the City lost the case? While everybody speculated on the outcome of the trials, boycotters were praying that the cases would be thrown out.

The day of Dr. King's trial, I, along with some 500 Negroes, including many of the boycotters who had been arrested, attended. There was no fear, anger, or bitterness. Everybody was together! We, the boycotters, occupied as many of the seats in the audience as we could. Many more people stayed outside and waited until the rest of us could come out and tell them what was going on.

Dr. King was brought into the courtroom by the authorities and given a seat where all could see him. He looked around and smiled as he saw how many of his church members and friends were there to support him. He was composed and seemingly felt quite comfortable as he waited for his trial to begin. Coretta, his wife, was there and smiled at him quite often. His lawyers were there, too—local lawyers and NAACP lawyers. Their composure, their facial expressions of assurance, dignity, preparation, readiness gave strength and assurance to the boycotters and to Dr. King and his wife. They knew that all was going well!

Perhaps in my prejudice I saw what I wanted to see, but I felt with strong conviction that the state lawyers were surprised, a bit shocked and taken off guard by the leadership of the opposition. They seemed a bit slow getting started.

While lawyers made preparation for the case at hand, Dr. King sat calmly, waiting. Sometimes he looked at his church members and friends, but often at his wife. He smiled at them. The smile showed confidence, fearlessness, faith. He seemed ready.

The NAACP lawyers and the local MIA lawyers had already gotten together and mapped out procedures, for only those lawyers on both sides who were approved by the court could participate in the trial. Seeing the competence of our outstanding black lawyers and the white lawyer Clifford Durr, we knew that all would be well. However, we had been informed by our lawyers that Dr. King certainly would be found guilty of leading and contributing to the boycott. Lawyers knew it and expected it, and so did Dr. King.

Montgomery Circuit Court Judge Eugene Carter presided over the trial, which began on March 19. Dr. King's defense attorneys included Arthur Shores of Birmingham, who had represented Miss Authurine Lucy in her attempt to enter the University of Alabama; Peter Hall of Birmingham; Orzell Billingsley; Fred Gray; Charles Langford; and Robert Carter, of the New York City NAACP's legal staff. The attorneys requested a non-jury trial. Among 77 witnesses summoned to testify were Mayor W. A. Gayle; Commissioners Frank Parks and Clyde Sellers; Police Chief G. J. Ruppenthal; former Police Commissioner Dave Birmingham; former Public Works Commissioner George Cleere; the bus company manager, J. H. Bagley; seven bus drivers who told of incidents of violence during the first days of the boycott; Erna Dungee, MIA financial secretary; Reverend A. W. Wilson; Mrs. Georgia Gilmore; Reverend Robert S. Graetz; *Advertiser* City Editor Joe Azbell; Ernest Smith, Negro janitor at the courthouse; and Beatrice Smith, a Negro woman who testified that a man whose name she did not know beat and knifed her because she insisted on continuing to ride buses.

MIA bookkeeping records and photostatic copies of bank deposit slips and checks introduced as evidence showed that the MIA had disbursed $30,713.80 for transportation services and other association expenses during the boycott. Eight service stations had received total amounts ranging from $300 to $1,318. Seventeen individuals had been paid a standard $24.00 a week for driving automobiles for the MIA. Several other people were confirmed as receiving compensation for related service in transportation.

After several days of anxious waiting, the decision was reached. Based on the boycott law, Judge Carter found Dr. King guilty of boycotting city buses. Nobody was surprised when he was found guilty. Prepared persons signed Dr. King's bond, and he was free on bail.

The guilty verdict made thousands of boycotters guilty, too, until their trials were determined. But there was never another trial of boycotters. Not one of those arrested, except for Dr. King, was ever ordered to stand trial or to pay a fine for boycotting. People kept waiting, and the pickup system that gave all boycotters rides kept operating. Nobody cared if the buses never ran again!

The lawyers for the boycotters had anticipated a guilty verdict and had told us to be prepared. They also had assured us that they were prepared to take the case to the federal court. They were firm in their belief that Dr. King and all the boycotters would be exonerated. With the hope the lawyers gave us, everybody kept high spirits, joyful attitudes, and faith in the lawyers. We all felt that the future would bring justice to all, regardless of race, creed, or color. Thus, everybody began looking toward the federal courts, waiting anxiously for the hearing and the decision that would be handed down.

The Last Mile

Almost four months had passed since December 5, 1955. Every plan the City Fathers had proposed to end the boycott had failed. Most of Montgomery's buses stood dusty and empty where they had been parked at Christmas. The MIA had developed its own free transportation service. There was a general belief that the situation could and would go on indefinitely.

The MIA continued to receive funds from all parts of the U.S.

and many places abroad. People from across the world still came to see and write about the situation.

Each Monday night thousands of people attended the weekly mass meetings. Collections were always taken, and every person who could contributed religiously and generously of her or his earnings to operate the transportation services. All of us who had steady jobs continued to give a percentage of our earnings each week, as we had since the beginning of the boycott. Drivers were paid regularly and were satisfied with their salaries. The station wagons had to be kept in good repair; fuel bills were enormous. The more money we needed, the more people, locally and elsewhere, seemed to give. The giving, the sharing, the serving continued on throughout the spring, summer, and fall of 1956. By April it was clear that the bus company and Montgomery's City Fathers had realized that black Americans meant it when they said they would never return to the buses except on an integrated basis, for all other efforts to get city buses rolling again had failed. Then our case in the federal courts began to move forward.

On May 11, a three-judge federal court, sitting in the federal courthouse in downtown Montgomery, heard arguments in the MIA's suit seeking a declaration that racially segregated seating on city buses violated the 14th Amendment's guarantee of equal government treatment of all citizens, irrespective of race, as the Supreme Court already had ruled on with regard to schools in its 1954 landmark opinion in *Brown* v. *Board of Education of Topeka*.

Several weeks later, on June 5, the judges announced that they had voted two to one against the constitutionality of segregated seating on Montgomery's city buses. Relegating black riders to the rear of city buses, or forcing them to stand over empty seats reserved for whites, or making them surrender seats to white passengers, were all unconstitutional practices.

Judge Richard T. Rives wrote the 2-to-1 majority decision. U.S. District Court Judge Frank M. Johnson joined him in the majority opinion. Their opinion struck down as unconstitutional the statutes requiring racially segregated seating on city buses.

After their opinion, the two judges were deluged for months

with hate mail, abusive telephone calls, and threats from segregationists for the stand they took and the opinion they gave that helped
to wipe out segregation. Old friends no longer spoke to them. Black
Montgomerians, however, will never forget either Rives or Johnson.

Montgomery city officials, though, did not celebrate or wel-
come Rives' and Johnson's ruling. Instead, they announced they
would appeal the decision to the U.S. Supreme Court. Five months
passed without any resolution of the matter. The city's buses remained segregated, and the MIA's transportation system continued
to function most effectively. Then, in mid-November, just as the
City Commission, under prodding from local segregationists, moved
in state court to enjoin the operation of our carpool system, the U.S.
Supreme Court issued a brief but decisive order, upholding Rives'
and Johnson's ruling that Montgomery's buses had to be integrated.
We thought at first that the change would take effect immediately,
but then learned, to our dismay, that the order would be effective
only when formally served on Montgomery officials. The City Commission, however, seeking to postpone as long as possible the arrival
of that order, petitioned the Supreme Court to reconsider its ruling.
The court rejected that request, but the legal maneuvering delayed
matters for several weeks, and it was not until Thursday, December
20, that U.S. marshals formally served the Supreme Court order on
city officials. That night the MIA held two mass meetings, and the
next morning Montgomery City Lines resumed full service on all
routes. Among its first passengers of the day were Mrs. Parks, Dr.
King, and Reverend Abernathy, who boarded an early morning bus
and took seats in what had once been the reserved, whites-only section as news photographers snapped pictures of the historic event.

The Sober Victory

At last, after thirteen long months, the boycotters had won. It was
terrible to watch women and children weep, hearing the news, and
even more awful to see grown black men stand and cry until their
whole bodies shook with bitter memories of the past. For now it was

all over—all those years of inhuman suffering, of brutality, arrests, and fines. The worst part of all had been their own helplessness in the face of it all! But now it was over.

The victory, however, brought no open festivities, no public rejoicing in the streets, no crowds milling on corners or around the leaders' homes. Too many people had suffered too much to rejoice. Too many people had lost their jobs.

Remembering that day many years later (*Advertiser*, February 24, 1982), Rosa Parks said, "I don't recall that I felt anything great about it. It didn't feel like a victory, actually. There still had to be a great deal to do." When newsmen persuaded her at the time of the victory to ride the buses and pose for pictures, "One of the drivers was the same one who had me arrested. He didn't react at all, and neither did I."

After the verdict sank in, the initial outbursts subsided, tears were wiped away, voices grew calm. In a few minutes the outward emotions disappeared, to be replaced by a prayerful attitude. Silent prayers of thanksgiving were uttered. A calm serenity spread over most faces.

Suddenly there was no more bitterness toward those bus drivers, toward the police, toward the system. In fact, there was even pity for the white people who had been so bitterly opposed to integration of the buses. We knew that *their* suffering at that moment was great, no matter the cause, and many religious black citizens breathed a prayer for those white people who were taking the court's decision with such difficulty. Other white citizens, who had been with the boycotters all the way, rejoiced now, of course.

At the beginning, black bus boycotters had learned to hate, and they had hated "with a vengeance." But they learned one thing: hate does more harm to the hater than to the hated. The body, the state of mind of the one hating responds to the hate, and, like an illness, the hate begins a deterioration of that body, that mind. Illness, even death, can result.

All boycotters learned this lesson. Dr. King had taught them that love is *redemptive*. That is why, thought they had continued to boycott, they had dismissed the bus drivers from their thinking. They learned to guide their thoughts to pleasant things. This was why they stopped "bugging whitey," why they laughed so much as they walked, why they could boycott for thirteen months while still working at their jobs and keeping their children in school, their bills paid, and their bodies well. Hate destroys, but love revitalizes!

When the announcement came that the boycott had officially ended, then, black citizens were too tired to gloat, to lose their dignity in public rejoicing. The time was too sacred, the need prayerful, the masses tearful and filled with thanksgiving. For God had led them through the wilderness of discrimination and abusive treatment.

The day had come when they could board a bus for downtown, or anywhere else, without fear of harassment. Never again would they have to be insulted or made to give up their seats to others because of the color of their skin. They could pay their fare as others did, take a seat, go to their destinations by bus with dignity and respect, and be treated as human beings!

At first the news provoked yells, loud exclamations of joy. But it seemed sacrilegious. Sometimes, on occasions such as this, I feel that loud laughter and rejoicing over others' defeat are out of place. I felt that way this time. I felt the need of prayer, the need to offer prayers of thanks to the superior spirit within me. Rejoicing publicly was not in my thoughts. We had come too far, suffered too much, for laughter. I did not call anybody, neither the MIA nor the WPC. And those of us who were together seemed almost simultaneously to grow quiet, prayerful. Some of us cried in thankfulness to God. I began to ignore the telephone, which was ringing continuously. I got quiet and still. After a while a great feeling of thankfulness, of freedom, of love for everybody inundated me. We black Americans were "free at last."

After the period of rejoicing, the WPC held a meeting and all members had recommendations to make, suggestions of policies to live by, and ideas to execute. The WPC would continue to operate, but the role of service would expand to the younger set, who would be including others in the planning. Members felt that young, concerned women, with their futures ahead, would benefit by the WPC, and that we would help them to organize and select goals and directions for their future. We did this, and two, maybe three groups of young women organized clubs in the name of the WPC.

9

The Aftermath

Although the first two months following the desegregation of Montgomery's buses witnessed a number of acts of white violence designed to discourage both blacks and whites from patronizing the integrated vehicles, by the spring of 1957 things seemed to settle down. The city seemed at peace for a time, and things were normal and quiet.

Buses rolled again, but few riders, white or black, patronized them with any great eagerness. In thirteen months, which had seemed an eternity, the bus patrons had gotten used to their interim transportation arrangements. Slowly more and more white passengers began riding. Also as time passed, the black masses gradually returned to the buses. A semblance of normality began to develop.

All passengers sat where they pleased without incident, and many of the black riders stated that a number of young white men and women smiled at them, and the black passengers smiled back. Most of them expressed surprise at the quiet on buses. People were not talking as much or as loudly as before. There was a quiet dignity among the black riders, for they had attained a sophistication while boycotting the buses, and they boarded them again with poise and dignity, their heads held high, their voices low, their manner stately. Many of the elderly boycotters felt that the black masses had really grown up in dignity, self-composure, and reserve. Dignity seemed to prevail with almost everyone.

The drivers, too, were minding their own business, driving the vehicles and not worrying about where black or white passengers sat. Many were just happy to have their jobs back. They were courteous as whites and blacks sat together, often conversing with each other as if that had always been done. By the time warm weather returned, almost all of the former riders began to patronize the buses again. And so the thirteen months of bitter experience were past.

Long after the boycott had ended, Mrs. Hazel Gregory and Mrs. Erna Dungee remained at the MIA headquarters, trying to help develop the old MIA organization into an institution for service to the people of Montgomery.

At Alabama State College

After some time had passed, between 1958 and 1960, news spread that some of the teachers at Alabama State College, who supposedly had been supporters of the boycott, were being investigated by a special state committee. I was still teaching at Alabama State College when this took place. These tensions were heightened in the spring of 1960, when some of our students "sat in" at the Montgomery County courthouse's segregated snack bar and were arrested. As the political pressures on the college increased, I resigned in the summer of 1960 and accepted a teaching position elsewhere.

The first professor affected was the chairman of the history department, Dr. Lawrence D. Reddick. A scholar interested in preserving historical documents for future generations, he had attended many sessions of the boycott movement on Monday nights, recording data for a biography of Dr. King, *Crusader Without Violence* that was published in 1959. Reddick was tried in absentia, without a hearing, we were informed, and was never given the opportunity to defend himself or to ascertain why he was being terminated. Instead, he was ordered by state officials to "leave the campus of Alabama State College and the City of Montgomery!"

Also in trouble was the brilliant English teacher, founder and staunch supporter of the WPC, Dr. Mary Fair Burks. Her crime was that she manifested interest in making conditions better for people to live creatively and prosperously, by becoming involved and helping to improve conditions. Like me, she also chose to resign in 1960.

During those years the power of the presidency was taken from Dr. Trenholm by white state officials, although he remained the president in name. All of us teachers at the college began having evaluators from the state's education department visit our classrooms. They sat taking notes all during the class periods. This went on for some time, though nothing explicitly came of it, as far as I know. Teachers did not seem to mind, however, though all knew that the move was one of intimidation. The teachers' records, which had been requested earlier, must have been satisfactory, for after 1960 no more teachers were dismissed, no students were expelled, and the college family breathed a sigh of relief when the ordeal was over.

However, the boycott had affected everyone at Alabama State. There had been mental strain on the administration, the faculty, and the student body. Dr. Trenholm had suffered as a result of the boycott, though he had not been directly involved. Many of the teachers, including myself, were weary. We had been loyal to the institution, to Dr. Trenholm, to our profession. We were not subversive. We had just gotten tired of being second-class citizens!

In 1960, on the last day of the spring semester, a large number of faculty members, some of whom had taught at Alabama State for thirty years (I had been there for eleven), resigned. Oddly enough, not one of us knew that the others were resigning. Time hadn't permitted us to talk to each other. None of us had other jobs in hand at the time. But we felt that insecurity was better than these jobs, which were proving a constant threat to our peace of mind. We knew, too, that we were well-trained, experienced, with excellent records, and that we could get other jobs.

I have held many excellent jobs, and every one I held, I left of my own accord. I learned very early that brazen arguments get one nowhere. Thus, I took the meek way, the one of humility. I gave my students my best. When I left, I showed my gratitude for serving on the staff as a faculty member.

With regret Dr. Trenholm accepted our resignations. The *Ad-*

vertiser's city editor, Joe Azbell, heard about the resignations and came to the college and talked with Dr. Trenholm. He requested the names of all the teachers resigning, their fields of concentration, and their years of service at the college. Dr. Trenholm authorized his secretary to give him that information. Before that evening had passed, Mr. Azbell had put this information about the resigning teachers on the wire service that carried news over much of the country. By eleven o'clock that night, every one of us who had resigned had been offered a job over the telephone at another college or university, at higher salaries, and with better opportunities for advancement. I cannot remember one who was without work.

I was offered two jobs. One was as chairperson of the English department of a new high school that had just been completed in Florida. The other position was in the English department at Grambling College in Louisiana; this job I accepted, because it was on the same level on which I had taught for the past twelve years.

I was the first of the group to leave. The semester ended on a Friday and I left the next day after bidding adieu to Dr. and Mrs. H. C. Trenholm, who had been my friends. Dr. Trenholm expressed regret at my leaving, but he did not try to persuade me to stay. He understood! I had worked untiringly to make that boycott a success, and it had been. We had worked diligently together, but we had had a difficult year. We had given our best to that boycott and to Alabama State. And in that last school year, 1959–60, we had given everything we had to carry on the college programs at a high level of quality despite the growing state political pressures. Students had advanced in experience and in education; the institution had braved the storm, for devoted teachers had kept it from sinking. There was no question of loyalty. For eleven years, from 1949 to 1960, I had given all I possessed in terms of learning and energy to the people of Alabama State College. Now it was just time to move on.

As I was leaving, I felt that my contribution was the beginning of a great period in the life of Alabama State College. I had never been happier. The boycott was successful. When I resigned there and left for Louisiana, I felt relaxed, for the memory of the boycott was behind me.

I liked Grambling, the students, and most of all, the teachers.

They were lovely people to work with, and to be around. I loved everybody there. However, after a few months had passed, I realized that the boycott had robbed me of something! It had taken its toll on my ability to adapt to new environments, new situations, new people. I began to feel lonely at Grambling, though the faculty and student body were wonderful to me. I seemed to adjust quickly, but to feel lonely afterward.

Christmas at home with my relatives was not much better; I felt lonely there, too. Back at Grambling, I really became involved and participated in everything. I thought I had overcome my loneliness. The second semester passed, and summer came. I decided to spend my summer in Los Angeles, where I had friends. For some reason I found myself in the office of the Los Angeles Board of Education, where I was offered a job teaching English in the public school system. I accepted it, found a house I could live with for a year, and sent for my furniture. I resigned from Grambling and moved to California. I worked there until I retired in 1976. By that time I had taught a total of thirty-five years, in five states—Georgia, Texas, Alabama, Louisiana, and California.

I did indeed miss Montgomery. Every time somebody from Alabama came to Los Angeles, they visited me. Two Alabama State faculty members, who had been there since my time, spent a night with me just a few years ago. They were still at Alabama State! But they talked about those of us who left, with kind memories of our contribution to Montgomery and the college. But it was predestined that I leave there, and after one year at Grambling College come to Los Angeles. It was in the cards.

When I retired, I bought myself six rental apartments. At present I am comfortably situated and actively engaged in civic and social work. After my retirement I gave one day of free service per week to the Los Angeles city government. I am active in the city's League of Women Voters; Alpha Kappa Alpha Sorority (Alpha Gamma Omega chapter); The Links (Angel City chapter); Black Women's Alliance; and the Founders Church of Religious Science. I am also a charter member of Women on Target. I do community work with a child care center, where I am especially interested in children with precocious minds. I have also worked with voter registration; and with senior citizens' assistance. I further occupy my time with contract bridge, keeping body and mind fit, and reading the best materials.

Those who stayed behind in Montgomery carried on what we had begun, as they should have. Since 1957, the WPC members, now retired and scattered around the country in various walks of life, still feel that a woman's duties do not end in the home, church, or classroom. Members have sought to determine the ills of dissatisfied black people and, through intelligent approaches to proper sources, to find solutions to the nagging problems that turn good men into beasts and kill the hopes, dreams, and faith of those who would strive toward something better.

The MIA is still a viable organization, though basically local. It is affiliated with the Southern Christian Leadership Conference, which Dr. King helped found in 1957 and which he headed until his death in 1968. For a number of years now, Mrs. Johnnie Carr has been the MIA's president.

The once-segregated Alabama State College, which for many years accommodated only black students taught only by black teachers, is now Alabama State University, part of the State of Alabama's university system. There both black and white teachers are employed, and both black and white students seek higher education in their chosen fields. Although Dr. H. C. Trenholm died some time ago, his widow, Mrs. Portia Trenholm Jenifer, remains my good friend.

The Fate of Dr. Martin Luther King, Jr.

But what about Dr. Martin Luther King, Jr., the Montgomery Bus Boycott's spokesman and leader for thirteen months? When the boycott ordeal ended, he was happy at our achievement, but his joy was short-lived.

Some people who could pull up family roots and leave Montgomery left after the boycott. Some left the state of Alabama, seeking peace of mind in a new environment where scars of the boycott would heal, where new faces and new opportunities would eradicate the bitter experience of the past few years of boycotting.

Dr. King himself moved to Atlanta in early 1960 in order to devote more time and attention to SCLC. In all honesty, our separation probably meant relatively little to Dr. King. Yes, I had worked closely with him, but others had, too. Yes, I had been less afraid than most women, because I knew I could get teaching positions elsewhere. Yes, I supported him and was a help with the MIA, but others, men and women, had been, too.

Dr. King knew, as all of us knew, that many faculty members would be leaving Alabama State College. We had suffered too much, fought too hard. We were, of necessity, tired—just plain tired. He hated to see us go, for we all had endured so much together.

In some ways, Dr. King had done all that he could in Montgomery. It was time that he, too, moved on. It had to be in the plan, for everything worked toward that end!

In 1960 he and his family moved to Atlanta, where Dr. King joined his father as co-pastor of the Ebenezer Baptist Church. Thanks to that arrangement, Dr. King was able to devote more energy to building and redeveloping the Southern Christian Leadership Conference. That organization enabled him to reach out to the masses, to help black people to aim for goals that were available to them. In the spring of 1961, Reverend Ralph Abernathy also moved from Montgomery to Atlanta to join Dr. King in leading the SCLC. Dr. King's expanding role enabled him to work with ministers in Birmingham, Nashville, and elsewhere throughout the southern states to help improve conditions for their people.

Along with other ministers who had dedicated their lives to helping to make the South a better place for all people to live in, Dr. King was soon engaged in a peaceful campaign of demonstrations in Birmingham in 1963. The protests were violently suppressed by police, using dogs and fire hoses.

Dr. King spent much of his time in Birmingham, often staying at the A. G. Gaston Motel. Shortly after the height of the protests, his motel headquarters was bombed, as was the home of his brother, the Reverend A. D. King. He was known, respected, and loved by many, yet he was feared by those who sought to prevent him from persuading blacks to fight for their rights.

Dr. King was arrested in Birmingham and incarcerated for a time. While he was in jail, he wrote a long reply to eight Birmingham clergymen who had publicly criticized the demonstrations. Dr. King admonished them to become aware of the suffering, the injustices, the needs of the black people and of the poor and needy of whatever race. That "Letter from a Birmingham Jail" is a masterpiece of literature. It has been reproduced many times.

Several months later on a Sunday morning in September 1963, a powerful bomb exploded at Birmingham's Sixteenth Street Baptist Church, the site of many of the movement's rallies and mass meetings. Four young girls attending Sunday school were killed.

The children's deaths brought deep grief to all concerned Americans, black and white. The bombing was despicable, cowardly, merciless, inhuman. People all over the country wondered about the heartless people who could perpetrate such a crime.

Meanwhile, Dr. King, who grieved when people suffered, grieved over this tragedy. The deaths of those four little girls in the Birmingham church were constantly in his memory. This seemed to increase his desire to work harder toward making conditions better for everybody.

In March 1965, Dr. King's organization, the sclc, in conjunction with numerous black Alabamians, began voting rights demonstrations in Selma, Alabama, and announced a "Protest March" from Selma to Montgomery, the state capital. People would actually walk on U.S. Highway 80 from Selma to Montgomery, a distance of fifty miles, to draw national attention to Alabama's racially discriminatory voter registration practices.

The day for the march was set, and the several hundred participants set out eastward from Selma toward Montgomery. Before they had traveled hardly a mile, however, Alabama lawmen blocked their route. Then, after only a brief pause, those state troopers and sheriff's deputies attacked the peaceful, unsuspecting column of marchers. The attackers used cattle prods, whips, tear gas, and clubs. After the marchers retreated and bound up their wounds, Dr. King returned to Selma and organized further protests as outraged supporters of civil rights from all across the nation traveled to Selma to lend their witness to the marchers' cause. Following a federal court order and intervention by President Lyndon B. Johnson, a heavily-protected column of marchers started out on a successful and peaceful trek to Montgomery on March 21. Several months later, at President Johnson's urging, Congress passed the Voting Rights Act of 1965, which put into effect most of the voting rights reforms that Dr. King and his co-workers had sought.

After that great victory, Dr. King resumed his work. He traveled all over the South where suffering among the poor and black in particular was great. He worked to help everybody who needed help. Color made no difference to him.

Still working for improvements for black communities in particular, in 1968 he went to Memphis, Tennessee, to work with the black community for the betterment of wages and working conditions for black sanitation men. White opposition to the campaign was intense, and Dr. King made several visits to Memphis.

One of the ministers who was with Dr. King a few days before he was killed told me that Dr. King said to him, "Somebody among us will die here." Dr. King then began crying, asking God, if any one of the ministers had to be taken, to "let that person be me!" On April 4, 1968, he was shot and killed by an assassin's bullet.

The assassin, James Earl Ray, is still incarcerated in prison. One wonders why a man, whom Dr. King never knew, and who had never done anything worthwhile to help society, would take the life of a man who did so much! Whatever amount of money he may have hoped to receive for the murder was indeed a small sum for the despicable job he agreed to do.

The tragedies of the King family did not end there. Hardly a year later, Dr. King's brother, A. D., an active, well-trained, ingenious, young minister, drowned in his swimming pool, apparently by accident. Several years after that, Dr. King's mother, who was an accomplished musician and organist in her husband's church, was at the piano during a Sunday morning service, playing for the choir. Suddenly, she was shot and killed by a supposedly deranged black man, who was arrested and put in jail. Mrs. King had spent a lifetime serving others in her community and making people happy.

One day I discussed the tragic history of the King family with a southern white theologian. We shared our mutual grief, for he knew that I had worked closely with Dr. King. This man had spent much time trying to find answers to such bitter outcomes as these that had happened to the King family. I, too, had spent hours in meditation and prayer, trying to reason why!

Trying to get his emotions together, he said to me, "It's not how long one lives, but how well one lives." His voice choked, and he stopped for a moment, waiting for me to speak. His eyes pleaded for me to say something, something that would help him. I immediately sensed that he was burdened with shame that the killers of Dr. King were probably white; that he and his race were, in some sense, guilty of this murder. But what about A. D.'s drowning, Mrs. King's murder? Neither of those deaths had been the work of whites.

I, too, was depressed and could not answer, for I needed answers, just as many other people throughout the country and the world needed answers that would comfort them. I remained silent, looking at him tearfully, with a questioning expression on my face, waiting for him to continue. I, too, needed answers concerning the fate of this beloved family.

After a moment he picked up where he had left off. "It's not how long one lives, but how well he lives in rendering service to mankind. For, you see," he said, looking at me, "death is not the end of life, but is the beginning of another life." After a pause, he went on. "These people have rendered more service during their short lives than some who live to be a hundred. They gave so much, so much of themselves, and had so much to offer . . ." He faltered, cleared his throat, tried to regain his composure. "And the ones who have robbed them of their chance to serve . . . do nothing to help others . . ." His voice choked, his eyes filled, and for a moment he stood there, fighting the tears. Then, overcome with grief, he reached out and grasped my hand. He muttered almost inaudibly, "God only knows." Then he let go of my hand, stood there in silence for a moment as if he were saying a prayer, and hurriedly walked away.

I stood there and watched that man until his tall, lanky, grieving figure was out of sight. And longer, for suddenly I realized that I was still standing there, staring at a figure who was no longer in sight. As I walked toward my destination I could not help but wonder how the killers of such wonderful people were doing. Had they forgotten? Would they ever forget? And the surviving members of the King family, whose lives would never be completely free of the memory of these terrible tragedies, would they be all right? Would they be able to let go and let God?

For I, too, had asked myself a hundred times and more why this lovely Christian family, highly intelligent, well-educated, with so much to offer the world, should be singled out for such undeserved grief and loss. I felt angry, and even silently asked the question, "Where was God?" I was immediately ashamed of my lack of faith.

I remember one of Dr. King's favorite readings, by an unknown author. I think of it as an epitaph for him: "Every child born should strive to fulfil his commitment to life. Every child has a talent; he should use it. Every child has a soul; he should cherish it. Every child has a mind; he should develop it." For Dr. King often quoted a philosopher who lived many years ago and who said: "A mind is a terrible thing to waste!" This latter slogan became the motto of the United Negro College Fund.

Dr. King's wife, Coretta Scott King, and their four children still live in Atlanta. The eldest child, Yolanda, who was two months old when the Kings' home was bombed, received a Master of Fine Arts degree in acting from New York University. She was a founding member of NUCLEUS, a company of performing artists dedicated to exploring and presenting ideas that will encourage and stimulate positive growth within humanity. She also serves on the board of directors of the Martin Luther King, Jr. Center for Nonviolent Social Change, where she is coordinator of the King Center's Cultural Institute.

I have always kept in touch with the Kings. Coretta and I are good friends. All the Kings are carrying on in Martin Luther King's footsteps, trying to make America a better place in which *all* people may live.

Today, in 1986, Montgomery is still the capital of the State of Alabama. It is still a beautiful city. But it is an integrated city. The population, black and white, remains about 250,000, but that population now is made up of free, proud people, white and black. The city enjoys public bus service on an integrated basis, as if the system had always been that way.

The cafeterias, where delicious southern-style foods were once served to whites only, are now open to all races. And instead of losing customers, such places have increased their clientele. Black Alabamians who are financially able to buy property in once-forbidden areas of the city may buy homes now, and "color" is less of a barrier. The city as a whole, instead of losing prestige, popularity, and visitation by people from across the country and the world, has gained in these areas.

Since December 1955, there has been a new attitude among black people in Montgomery. They seem to recognize, now more than ever, that freedom is bought with a price, that nothing of value comes easily. Black people seem less afraid and more willing to pay the price for striving forward. As Dr. King often preached from his pulpit, "suffering is redemptive." Perhaps that logic of acceptance has nowhere been proved more effective than in the case of black Montgomerians, for they are a new people!

Professor J. E. Pierce believed that black people had largely overcome the inferiority complex that had been forced upon them through more than a hundred years of subjection. Today they understand that all jobs are honorable if they are honest; that a maid is as indispensable as a merchant; that a well-kept home is as important as an office; that a factory is no more important than a farm. "Any one of these," Professor Pierce said, "is totally dependent upon the others!" The new Negro, then, is quite different. In Montgomery, he changed almost overnight, so to speak. In Professor Pierce's words, the new black in Alabama is "confident, proud, calm, firm, and unafraid!"

Yet continuing frequent public announcements by the Ku Klux Klan or other "hate" groups prove that prejudice is still around, not only in Alabama but in Georgia, Florida, and even California. The demons of racial hatred are much alive and are, seemingly, everywhere.

All Americans are human beings, despite color. Color is only skin deep, and all blood is red. Underneath every person's skin is a heart, a soul, a mind, and a conscience, with which every human being is endowed. Thus, a person should not and cannot be measured by the color of his skin or the texture of his hair but, to quote Dr. King, "by the quality of their character."

That being the case, the world would be a much better place if, beginning tomorrow and throughout eternity, as Dr. King envisioned, every nation tried to recognize the brotherhood of man and the fatherhood of God. Dr. King was interested in "human recognition." If we all tried to recognize the humanity of every living being, this would be a better world.

No man is free until all men are free! White Americans, yes! But black Americans, too! And brown Americans, yellow Americans, and red Americans. All are still fighting for full citizenship rights. Gains have been made in each case. However, equal opportunities do not exist in every part of America for everyone. Someday they will! Dr. George Washington Carver touched the core of democracy years ago when he said to Mrs. Mary McLeod Bethune:

> This land is ours by right of birth;
> this land is ours by right of toil.
> We helped to turn its virgin earth;
> our sweat is in its fruitful soil.
>   —Brander Matthews, *To Make a Poet Black*

America was built upon struggle, in which all Americans participated. And in the struggle for equality in Montgomery, Alabama, all people there participated. That is why the Montgomery story must be told. And so it has been.

Glossary of Individuals

Rev. Ralph D. Abernathy.   Pastor, First Baptist Church, and later
    vice president, Montgomery Improvement Association.
Mr. Joe Azbell.   City editor, *Montgomery Advertiser.*
Mr. J. H. Bagley.   Manager, Montgomery City Lines, Inc.
Mrs. Maude Ballou.   Personal secretary to Dr. Martin Luther King, Jr.
Rev. L. Roy Bennett.   Vice president, MIA.
Mr. Dave Birmingham.   Montgomery city commissioner, 1953–1955.
Mr. P. M. Blair.   The "bronze mayor" of Montgomery; a black leader fa-
    vored by white Montgomery.
Mr. James F. Blake.   Montgomery City Lines bus driver who, on De-
    cember 1, 1955, requested the arrest of Mrs. Rosa Parks.
Mrs. Aurelia S. Browder.   Lead plaintiff in the MIA's federal court suit
    seeking desegregation of Montgomery's buses.
Dr. Mary Fair Burks.   Founder of the Women's Political Council; professor
    and head of the English department, Alabama State College.
Mr. Mac S. Butler.   Sheriff of Montgomery County.
Mr. John Cannon.   Head of the business department, Alabama State
    College.
Judge Eugene Carter.   The magistrate who presided over the grand jury
    investigation of the MIA and the trial of Dr. King.
Mr. George Cleere.   Montgomery commissioner of public works,
    1953–1955.
Dr. M. C. Cleveland.   Pastor, Day Street Baptist Church.
Miss Claudette Colvin.   An early, pre-boycott victim of Montgomery's bus
    segregation practices whose arrest stimulated black protests about
    the discrimination.

Mr. Q. P. Colvin.   Claudette's father and party to the MIA's federal court suit.

Mr. Jack Crenshaw.   Attorney for the Montgomery City Lines.

Mrs. Erna Dungee (later Allen).   Financial secretary, MIA.

Mr. Clifford Durr.   White Montgomery lawyer helpful to boycotters.

Rev. Uriah J. Fields.   Pastor, Bell Street Baptist Church, and the first recording secretary of the MIA.

Mr. James E. Folsom.   Governor of Alabama, 1955–1958.

Rev. E. N. French.   Pastor, Hilliard Chapel AME Church, and corresponding secretary, MIA.

Mr. W. A. Gayle.   Mayor of Montgomery, 1951–1959.

Mrs. Georgia Gilmore.   A solid, energetic boycott participant and supporter.

Mrs. Thelma Glass.   An active member of the WPC.

Rev. Robert S. Graetz.   A young white pastor of a black congregation, who actively supported the boycott and suffered extensive harassment as a result.

Mr. Fred D. Gray.   Young, black Montgomery lawyer who represented and led the MIA.

Mrs. Hazel Gregory.   Office secretary, MIA.

Mr. Grover C. Hall, Jr.   Editor of the *Montgomery Advertiser*.

Dr. Richard "Rick" Harris.   Pharmacist; owner of Dean's Drugstore, one of two key downtown pickup stations for the MIA carpool.

Dr. Vernon Johns.   Activist pastor of the Dexter Avenue Baptist Church in the years prior to Dr. King.

Mrs. Martha Johnson.   Secretary-clerk, MIA.

Mr. Tom Johnson.   *Montgomery Advertiser* reporter who covered the boycott.

Dr. Moses W. Jones.   Boycott activist and later an officer of the MIA.

Mrs. Coretta Scott King.   Wife of Dr. Martin Luther King, Jr.

Dr. Martin Luther King, Jr.   Pastor, Dexter Avenue Baptist Church, and president, Montgomery Improvement Association.

Mr. R. L. Lampley.   Montgomery city fire chief.

Mr. Charles Langford.   Black Montgomery lawyer.

Mr. C. W. Lee.   Assistant treasurer, MIA.

Mr. Rufus A. Lewis.   President of the Citizens' Steering Committee, and the man who nominated Dr. King as president of the MIA.

Miss Juliette Morgan.   White Montgomery librarian.

Mr. Robert Nesbitt.   Leading officer of the Dexter Avenue Baptist Church and boycott activist.

Mr. E. D. Nixon.   President, Montgomery Progressive Democratic Association; former NAACP state president; treasurer, MIA.

Mr. Frank Parks.   Montgomery city commissioner, 1955–1957.

Mrs. Rosa Parks.   Well-respected Montgomery seamstress whose arrest sparked the bus boycott.

Professor James E. "Jim" Pierce.   Professor, Alabama State College, and key black Montgomery political activist, both before and during the boycott.

Mrs. Zoeline Pierce.   wpc member and wife of Professor J. E. Pierce.

Rev. W. J. Powell.   Pastor, Old Ship A. M. E. Zion Church, and a leading MIA member.

Mrs. Inez Ricks.   Organizer of the Friendly Club.

Mrs. Jo Ann Gibson Robinson.   President, Women's Political Council, and professor of English, Alabama State College.

Mr. Goodwyn J. Ruppenthal.   Montgomery city police chief.

Rev. S. S. Seay.   Committed black minister active in the boycott; later MIA executive secretary.

Mr. Clyde Sellers.   Police commissioner.

Mr. Arthur Shores.   Black Birmingham lawyer who assisted Dr. King and the MIA.

Rev. Thomas Thrasher.   Leading member of the Alabama Council on Human Relations and the man who arranged initial negotiations between the MIA and white officials.

Mr. K. E. Totten.   Official of National City Lines sent to study the Montgomery situation.

Dr. H. Councill Trenholm.   President, Alabama State College.

Mrs. Portia Trenholm.   Music teacher, Alabama State College, and wife of Dr. H. C. Trenholm.

Mrs. Irene West.   Key member of the wpc and MIA leadership, and wife of A. W. West, Sr.

Mr. Aubrey Williams.   One of the few white liberals and white MIA supporters in Montgomery.

Professor Robert Williams.   Music teacher at Alabama State College and close friend of Dr. King.

Rev. A. W. Wilson.   Pastor, Holt Street Baptist Church, and parliamentarian, MIA.

Chronology of Events

December 1, 1955.   Mrs. Rosa Parks arrested for refusing to give up her
seat on a Montgomery bus to a white man.

December 2, 1955.   Mrs. Jo Ann Robinson and other black Montgomery
activists begin working for a Monday, December 5 boycott of all
city buses.

December 5, 1955.   The first-day boycott is a huge success. An afternoon
black leadership meeting establishes the Montgomery Improvement
Association and elects Rev. Martin Luther King, Jr., as president.
An evening mass meeting resolves that the boycott will continue
until the MIA's three demands are met by white officials.

December 8, 1955.   The first meeting takes place between MIA leaders
and white city and bus company officials, and ends unsuccessfully
as the whites refuse to give serious consideration to the MIA's demand for changed seating practices on city buses.

Mid-December 1955 through mid-January 1956.   MIA's boycott of city
buses continues as whites refuse to grant concessions and MIA im-
proves its alternative transportation system for black Montgomerians.

Late January 1956.   Montgomery's white city commissioners announce a
new "get tough" policy toward the black boycott, and city police
begin harassing MIA carpool drivers.

January 30, 1956.   Dr. King's home is bombed.

February 1, 1956.   MIA attorney Fred Gray files a federal court suit chal-
lenging the constitutionality of segregated seating on Montgomery
city buses.

Early and mid-February 1956.   White businessmen negotiate unsuccessfully with the MIA for an end to the boycott while a grand jury

prepares to indict MIA leaders for allegedly violating a state anti-boycott law.

February 21, 1956.   Some ninety MIA activists are indicted under the state anti-boycott law.

March 19, 1956.   Dr. King's trial as the first boycott defendant begins; three days later King is convicted and fined $1,000. The MIA appeals as the national news media decries white Montgomery's conduct and the boycott of city buses continues with solid fervor.

May 11, 1956.   The one-day trial of the MIA's federal court suit against bus segregation takes place in Montgomery.

June 5, 1956.   By a 2-to-1 vote, the three federal judges who had heard the MIA's suit rule that bus segregation is unconstitutional. White city officials appeal the decision to the U.S. Supreme Court.

Summer and early fall 1956.   The MIA's boycott continues as both sides increasingly anticipate that the bus situation will be resolved only when the Supreme Court issues a definitive ruling on the bus segregation question.

October 30, 1956.   City officials move in state court to try to get the MIA's carpool system of alternative transportation abolished; a court hearing is set for November 13.

November 13, 1956.   As MIA leaders gather for the state court proceeding, the U.S. Supreme Court announces that it has affirmed the lower federal court ruling holding Montgomery's bus segregation unconstitutional. Integrated bus seating will begin once the court order is formally served on city officials.

December 20, 1956.   U.S. marshals officially serve the Supreme Court order on Montgomery officials.

December 21, 1956.   For the first time in over a year, black Montgomerians return to city buses and sit wherever they please as news photographers snap pictures showing the demise of segregated seating.

Index